Making
Chain Mail
Jewelry

Making
Chain Mail
Jewelry

Lauren Andersen

KALMBACH BOOKS

Kalmbach Books
21027 Crossroads Circle
Waukesha, Wisconsin 53186
www.Kalmbach.com/Books

Step-by-step photos by the author. All other photography © 2013 Kalmbach Books.

Published in 2013
17 16 15 14 13   1 2 3 4 5

Manufactured in the United States of America

ISBN: 978-0-87116-480-3
EISBN: 978-1-62700-060-4

Editor: Karin Van Voorhees
Art Director: Lisa Bergman
Technical Editor: Theresa D. Abelew
Illustrator: Kellie Jaeger
Photographers: William Zuback and James Forbes

Publisher's Cataloging-in-Publication Data

Andersen, Lauren.

  Making chain mail jewelry / Lauren Andersen.

  p. : col. ill. ; cm. — (The absolute beginners guide)

"Everything you need to know to get started."—Cover.

Issued also as an ebook.

ISBN: 978-0-87116-480-3

1. Chains (Jewelry)—Handbooks, manuals, etc. 2. Metal-work—Handbooks, manuals, etc. 3. Wire jewelry—Handbooks, manuals, etc. 4. Jewelry making—Handbooks, manuals, etc. I. Title. II. Title: Chain mail III. Title: Absolute beginners guide making chain mail jewelry IV. Series: Absolute beginners guide.

TT212 .A54 2013
745.594/2

Contents

Introduction

With two pairs of pliers and some jump rings, you can make gorgeous jewelry! Technically, chain mail or *maille* is a type of armor consisting of small metal rings linked together in a pattern to form a mesh. Beginning in the 5th century, the mesh was worn by soldiers to protect themselves from spears and sharp objects. Nowadays, chain mail is used for everything from mesh to protect butchers' hands from sharp blades, to cages to protect shark explorers from shark attacks, to my favorite—fabulous jewelry. This book will teach you every step in the process of making your own chain mail jewelry.

Chain mail is the art of connecting jump rings in a specific pattern, or weave, to create a fabric-like result. It's incredibly versatile: You can combine segments of a weave and incorporate your own beads, crystals, and clasps, to make a piece your own. Once you learn a few weaves, you will want to explore many more. You are only limited by your imagination!

This book begins with the Basics. You'll learn about common tools used in chain mail, how to open and close a jump ring properly, and how to set up your workspace. For chain mail supplies, the best starting place is always your local bead store.

Then, you'll learn the seven most common and useful chain mail weaves.

I suggest that you start with the first weave, the European 4-in-1, and then learn the weaves in order. Practice each weave by using the large colored rings listed. When you feel you have mastered the mechanics of the weave, try making the pictured piece of jewelry using the size and material jump rings listed in the "what you'll need" box.

Once you learn these seven weaves, it's on to the projects. If you already have experience with chain mail weaves, feel free to jump right to the projects.

The projects are your opportunity to have some creative fun! All of the projects use the basic chain mail weaves. Some add crystals or other unusual materials, such as the "thingy" that holds your glasses to a chain. If you get

stuck, you can always refer back to the weave instructions for a refresher.

At the end of the book, you'll find a Glossary of Terms Used in Chain Mail—a reference to some of the "insider language" you'll come across. This is not an exhaustive list of every chain mail term, but it will bring clarity to important terms such as *aspect ratio* and *springback*.

I've pulled everything you need to get started in this great hobby together in one source.

Are you ready?
Let's go.

You are only limited by
your imagination!

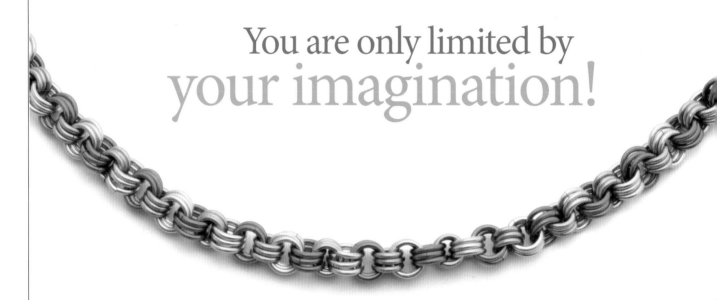

Basics

TOOLS

What tools do you need to get started making chain mail? This section will show you.

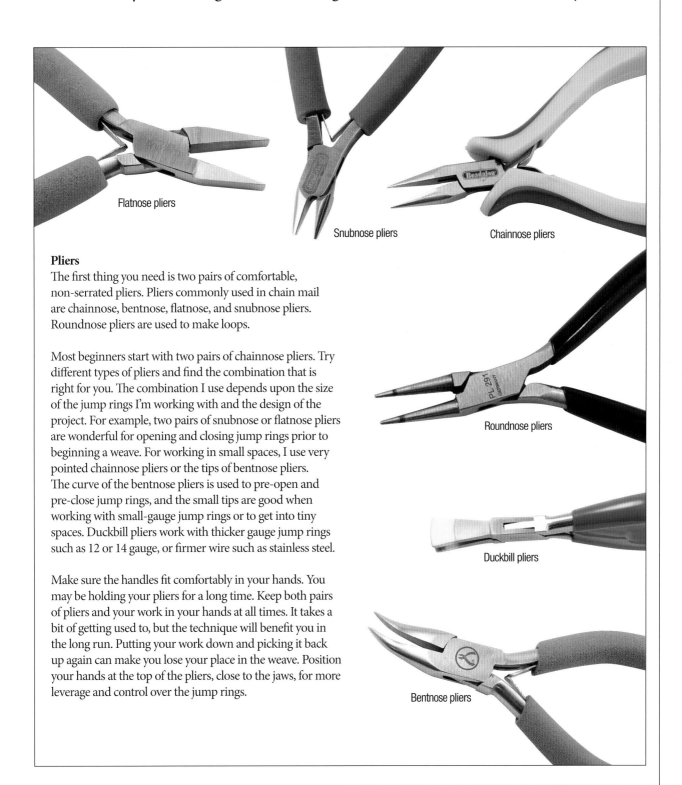

Flatnose pliers

Snubnose pliers

Chainnose pliers

Roundnose pliers

Duckbill pliers

Bentnose pliers

Pliers

The first thing you need is two pairs of comfortable, non-serrated pliers. Pliers commonly used in chain mail are chainnose, bentnose, flatnose, and snubnose pliers. Roundnose pliers are used to make loops.

Most beginners start with two pairs of chainnose pliers. Try different types of pliers and find the combination that is right for you. The combination I use depends upon the size of the jump rings I'm working with and the design of the project. For example, two pairs of snubnose or flatnose pliers are wonderful for opening and closing jump rings prior to beginning a weave. For working in small spaces, I use very pointed chainnose pliers or the tips of bentnose pliers. The curve of the bentnose pliers is used to pre-open and pre-close jump rings, and the small tips are good when working with small-gauge jump rings or to get into tiny spaces. Duckbill pliers work with thicker gauge jump rings such as 12 or 14 gauge, or firmer wire such as stainless steel.

Make sure the handles fit comfortably in your hands. You may be holding your pliers for a long time. Keep both pairs of pliers and your work in your hands at all times. It takes a bit of getting used to, but the technique will benefit you in the long run. Putting your work down and picking it back up again can make you lose your place in the weave. Position your hands at the top of the pliers, close to the jaws, for more leverage and control over the jump rings.

TOOLS

Beading awl
The beading awl helps to define the space where the next jump ring needs to go. I also use it to place the jump rings where I want them in the weave. It's a very handy tool for chain mail. (A stiff piece of wire works well, too.)

Beading mat
Just like the beading mat that helps keep your beads from scattering, chain mailers use a beading mat to keep jump rings under control. Beading mats are made from a non-linty material and they come in a variety of colors. You can use a piece of felt or even a towel for a mat, but be careful that the fibers aren't too prominent or they may catch on open rings.

Chain Mail Tray
I love this! Full disclosure: It's my invention. The Chain Maille Lady Travel Kit includes a case, two beading mats, and a flocked tray with a lip to keep jump rings in place. I work on one mat, and when I'm done, the other mat goes on top of my work, I attach the plastic top, and put it back in the travel kit.

Task lamp
Lighting is very important in chain mail. You need to see whether or not the jump rings are closed properly. A full-spectrum task light will enable you to see your work in the proper light. There are several types of task lighting. I suggest a portable task light so that you can bring it with you to a class. You can even find a task light that runs on batteries!

Cutters
Use flush cutters, diagonal wire cutters, or side cutters to trim off the ends of beading wire after crimping. Also use them to cut wire for loops.

Pliers coating
Dipping your pliers with a rubberized material or wrapping them with tape helps avoid marring your jump rings. Chain mailers often use a product called Tool Magic.

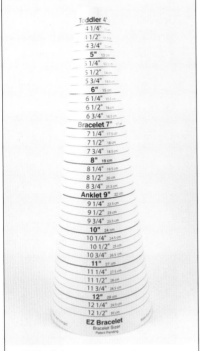

Bracelet measurer

A bracelet measurer is especially handy for bulky bracelet designs. If you place a bracelet flat and measure it with a measuring tape, it will be one length, but when you place it on the bracelet measurer, it will be up to an inch shorter. The circumference of the bracelet is actually smaller when you fit it around your wrist.

Magnification

Magnification is extremely important in chain mail. You will be surprised how much easier it is to see tiny little jump rings when you use a magnifier. You will need to have magnification that is hands-free: Choose from magnifiers that attach to your glasses, a set that can be secured around your head and pull down in front of your eyes, or a combination task light magnifier. Hands-free magnification is extremely helpful to make sure that you have completely and smoothly closed those jump rings.

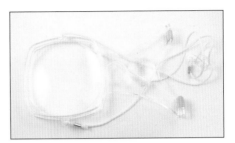

Bead Stopper

Use these with beading wire to hold a project in place.

Jump ring tool

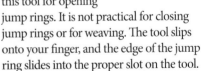

This tool can substitute for one pair of pliers. You only use this tool for opening jump rings. It is not practical for closing jump rings or for weaving. The tool slips onto your finger, and the edge of the jump ring slides into the proper slot on the tool.

Storage

I have labeled this eight-compartment storage container with the colors and sizes of the jump rings it holds. This is crucial! You must keep your jump rings separated. You can keep them in the packages they came in, as long as they are labeled, or you can transfer them to a storage container. Find a container with a lip on the lid to help keep the jump rings from migrating to other compartments. You do not want to mix your jump rings. I can't say this enough! Also list the gauge and the size (inside diameter) of the jump rings.

Basics

Trays
You will love these triangular bead trays for scooping up jump rings and returning them to their proper storage compartments.

Glue
Add a drop of glue to a knot to keep it from pulling apart.

Paper clips
A paper-clip handle comes in handy when you are beginning a weave.

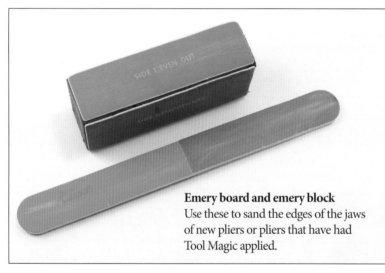

Emery board and emery block
Use these to sand the edges of the jaws of new pliers or pliers that have had Tool Magic applied.

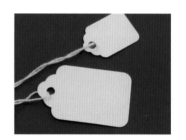

Jewelry tags
I write down the jump rings sizes, quantity, and type of metal I used in the design on tags. I also include the name of the piece.

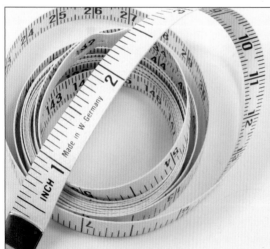

Flexible tape measure
Measure around your wrist to estimate the bracelet length, but be sure to put a finger or two between your wrist and the tape measure for a comfortable fit.

Goo Gone
If you tape your pliers' jaws to protect the jump rings, you'll need Goo Gone to remove any sticky residue from the pliers when you remove the tape. Rub it on with a paper towel.

MATERIALS

Chain mail weaves are made with small metal circles called jump rings. A jump ring is made by winding wire around a cylindrical metal rod (called a mandrel) to create a coil. The coil is then cut with a saw or wire cutters. Using a saw to cut the coil creates two smooth edges so the jump ring can be closed seamlessly. If wire cutters or flush cutters are used to cut the coil, the resulting jump rings will have what is known as *pinch-out*: one flat edge and one edge with a bur that looks like this <. Pinch-out jump rings will never fully close. To get a smooth edge with wire cutters, turn the blade and make a second cut to trim the pinch-out flush with the ring.

The jump ring on the right has been cut with flush cutters. It is very subtle but you can see that the left side of the cut is flat and the right side of the cut is "pinched" (<). The jump ring on the left has been saw-cut.

The gap between the two cut ends is called the *kerf*. See p. 14 for details about properly closing jump rings to eliminate kerf.

Jump rings come in many different sizes, metals, textures, and colors. Some of the most common metals used are sterling silver, Argentium silver, German silver, silver filled, silver plated, gold filled, niobium, enamel-coated copper, aluminum, copper, brass, and bronze. Rubber rings are also used for chain mail. All jump rings are not suitable for chain mail: a chain mail jump ring must be hard (or sturdy) enough to withstand use and wear and tear not just during construction, but also when the jewelry is worn by the lucky recipient. Flimsy jump rings increase the chance that the fabulous piece of jewelry you have spent so much time to make will come apart.

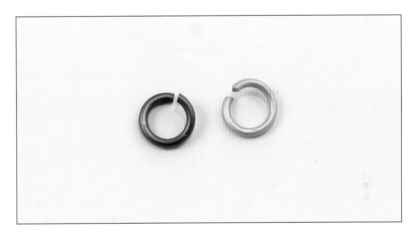

Jump rings
Enamel-coated copper
Brass
Copper
Silver
Anodized aluminum
Textured or patterned

Inner and outer diameter

In chain mail jump rings are measured using the inner diameter of the ring. In this book—and in most chain mail books—the ring diameter is the inner diameter. To convert outer diameter to inner diameter, multiply the wire diameter by two and then subtract the result from the outside diameter.

Mandrel Sizes	
INCH SIZE	MM SIZE
3/32"	2.38mm
7/64"	2.78mm
1/8"	3.18mm
9/64"	3.57mm
5/32"	3.97mm
11/64"	4.37mm
3/16"	4.76mm
13/64"	5.16mm
7/32"	5.56mm
15/64"	5.95mm

Wire gauge

There are two different wire gauge systems which represent the thickness of the wire used to make chain mail jump rings: American Wire Gauge (AWG) and Standard Wire Gauge (SWG). The AWG system is generally used for measuring precious metals such as sterling silver, gold, and niobium. SWG is generally used for measuring base metals such as aluminum, anodized aluminum, stainless steel, copper, brass, and enamel-coated copper rings.

Wire Gauges		
WIRE GAUGE	AWG	SWG
14	.064" (1.63mm)	.080" (2.03mm)
15	.057" (1.45mm)	.072" (1.83mm)
16	.051" (1.29mm)	.064" (1.63mm)
17	.045" (1.15mm)	.056" (1.42mm)
18	.040" (1.02mm)	.048" (1.22mm)
19	.036" (0.91mm)	.040" (1.02mm)
20	.032" (0.81mm)	.036" (0.91mm)
21	.028" (0.72mm)	.032" (0.81mm)

Components and Findings

Components and findings are all the clasps, crystals, beads, earring wires, and other things that will help turn your piece of chain mail into finished jewelry. You have the option to jazz your design up or keep it simple. You can change the whole look of a bracelet by adding a fancy clasp—maybe one with lots of bling! There are some unusual components in some of these projects. Feel free to substitute your own choices of beads, crystals, and earring wires.

Clasps
Toggle, lobster, slide, and box clasps.

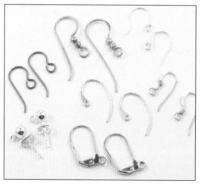

Earring wires
French style or hook, lever back, and post.

Bead stringing materials

Flexible beading wire is composed of multiple steel wires twisted together and nylon coated. The number of wires, or strands, determines the flexibility of the wire. The greater the number of strands the more flexible the wire will be. Bead stringing wire comes in 7, 10, 14, 19, 24, and 49 strands.

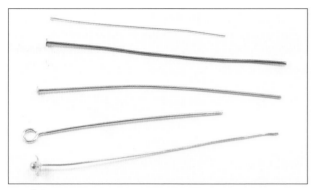

Headpins

Headpins are both functional (plain) and decorative (ball or crystal tipped). Headpins come in different lengths and sizes. You need enough wire above the top bead to make a plain or wrapped loop (p. 15). Eyepins have a pre-made loop on one end, which makes it easier to create beaded links.

Wire as it comes off the spool

When you purchase wire it will usually come in this form. This is silver-filled wire that I wind around a mandrel to create a coil, and then cut jump rings.

Seed beads

I use seed beads as spacers that will usually lie under a jump ring. This will leave a bit of wiggle room in your project and it will also evenly space your beads, crystals, or pearls.

Crimp beads, tubes, and loops

Crimp beads range in size from #1 (smallest) to #3 (largest). Crimp tubes are sized as #1, #2, and #3. Loop tubes are my favorite. I use them in all of my designs with strung crystals or beads where the beading wire will be attached to a jump ring, so the wire doesn't wiggle through the jump ring. The different crimp sizes allow you to crimp multiple bead stringing wires at once. Make sure that the crimp is large enough to accommodate at least two passes of the bead stringing wire.

Beads

Pearls

Crystals

TECHNIQUES

Working with Jump Rings
Opening and closing

This is the most important technique to master in chain mail. It takes practice, so do not expect to be an expert immediately. Jump rings from the package may look like they are open, but you must open them further or close them tightly in order to weave them into patterns.

It is a good idea to practice closing jump rings. Every jump ring will eventually need to be closed.

1. Place the pliers in your hands with your thumb and index finger as close to the jaws as is comfortable. This gives you more control and leverage.

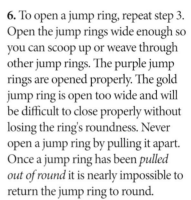

2. The jump ring looks like this when it comes out of the package: The distance or gap between the two cut ends of the jump ring is called the *kerf*. To close the gap, grasp the jump ring in the jaws of the pliers with the open area of the jump ring at the top and one pair of pliers' jaws on either side at about a 35- to 45-degree angle. If you grip too far down on the jump ring, you will not have the proper leverage.

3. Bring your dominant hand forward and your nondominant hand away from you, and at the same time, press the ends of the jump ring in toward each other. The inward pressure is critical to getting the jump ring completely closed. The inward motion closes the kerf. The ends of the jump ring will overlap slightly.

4. Reverse the motion performed in step 3 by bringing your non-dominant hand forward and your dominant hand back while pressing the ends of the jump ring inward toward each other. Notice how the ends again overlap.

5. Bring your dominant hand forward, and even out the ends of the jump ring. Wiggle the ends into position by pushing and pulling the ends in tiny motions for a seamless closure.

6. To open a jump ring, repeat step 3. Open the jump rings wide enough so you can scoop up or weave through other jump rings. The purple jump rings are opened properly. The gold jump ring is open too wide and will be difficult to close properly without losing the ring's roundness. Never open a jump ring by pulling it apart. Once a jump ring has been *pulled out of round* it is nearly impossible to return the jump ring to round.

Don't worry; you'll get lots of practice opening and closing jump rings!

Preparation

At the beginning of each project in this book, you are directed to open and close a specific number of jump rings. It is very helpful to pre-open and pre-close jump rings. The advance work means you don't need to stop the weave and open or close a bunch of jump rings. You will be able to concentrate on the weave itself.

Doubling the jump ring

When a second jump ring must follow the same path as the first jump ring, you'll be instructed to *double the ring*. An example is the Byzantine weave (p. 20). In some projects, you will be asked to triple the jump ring, or add two additional jump rings to the original path.

Beginning a weave with a handle

Having a handle—something to grasp while you begin the weave—is a tremendous help. The instructions may direct you to begin your weave directly from the clasp or earring wire (which becomes the handle). You can use a paper clip, a piece of chain, or even a twist tie as your starting place. When you begin a new weave, it may feel awkward, but don't worry—most chain mail weaves repeat the same steps over and over again. Some weaves take a few steps before stabilizing. I find the repetition of weaving very soothing.

Other Basics

There are some simple beading techniques that you'll use as you make chain mail jewelry. These include:

Plain loop

Use this technique to connect dangles when you will not be putting a lot of strain on the piece.

1. Trim the wire or headpin ⅜" (1cm) above the top bead. Make a right-angle bend close to the bead.

2. Grab the wire's tip with roundnose pliers. The tip of the wire should be flush with the pliers. Roll the wire to form a half circle. Release the wire.

3. Reposition the pliers in the loop and continue rolling.

4. The finished loop should form a centered circle above the bead.

Wrapped loop

I find this to be the most secure way to attach beads and crystals when dangling them from my chain mail.

1. String a crystal or bead on a headpin. With roundnose pliers, grasp the headpin just above the top of the bead, with the jaws of the pliers horizontal. I have marked my pliers with a red permanent marker so that my loops will be the same size.

2. Bend the headpin across the pliers at a 45-degree angle.

3. Rotate the pliers so they are vertical and one jaw is on top of the headpin wire and one jaw is between the top of the bead and the headpin wire.

4. Bend the headpin wire over the top of the top pliers' jaw and keep bending until the headpin wire touches the bead.

5. Adjust the pliers so that the lower jaw (previously between the bead and the headpin wire) is now in the curve of the headpin wire.

6. Bring the headpin wire around the bottom jaw of the pliers and up to a 45-degree angle to the bead. At this point, the loop can be connected to other components.

7. With one pair of chainnose pliers, grasp the loop, and with a second set of pliers, grab the wire tail. Begin to wrap the tail around the stem. I usually wrap halfway around and then readjust my pliers.

8. Wrap the wire tail until it touches the top of the bead. With a pair of flush cutters, cut the wire as close to the stem as you can. The loop is securely closed.

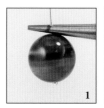

Flattened crimp

I like to use a flattened crimp in place of a loop crimp when space is tight and there is only room to get the tips of the pliers in to the space to crimp the crimp.

1. Hold the crimp using the tip of the chainnose pliers. Squeeze the pliers firmly to flatten the crimp.

2. Tug the wire to make sure the crimp has a solid grip. If the wire slides, repeat the step with a new crimp.

A Note about Aspect Ratio (AR)

In simple terms, the aspect ratio is a way of describing how thick or thin a jump ring is. You can make your weave open and airy or tight with no flexibility. When you make a piece of chain mail, you will notice that jump rings go inside other jump rings. Calculating the aspect ratio means figuring out how many jump rings each jump ring can comfortably hold.

The formula for finding the aspect ratio is: Inside diameter divided by wire diameter or

$$\frac{ID}{wire\ diameter} = AR$$

Before you slam the book shut and go screaming out of the room because you don't like math, let me assure you it is not necessary to know anything about aspect ratio to get started making chain mail from this book. The jump ring sizes you need to know are listed at the beginning of each project. I just want you to be aware that at some point aspect ratio may become important in your chain mail journey. Most vendors who sell chain mail supplies have a frequently asked questions (FAQ) section on their website that includes a section on aspect ratio.

WORKSPACE

One of the things I really love about chain mail is that it requires so few tools and it's so portable! You can pack up a travel kit and make chain mail just about anywhere, such as at a sporting event or a concert. Take it with you when you travel. Hop in your RV and chain mail on down the road, as long as you are not the driver.

Your workspace should include a chain mail tray with a beading mat, two pairs of your favorite pliers (mine are snubnose pliers), a tri-tray to pick up those pesky jump rings, task lighting and magnification, and a beading awl for those stubborn jump rings that just won't stay where you want them. Oh, and of course, jump rings! You'll use a setup like this in every project in the book. That's why I've omitted tools from the "What You'll Need" list at the beginning of each project.

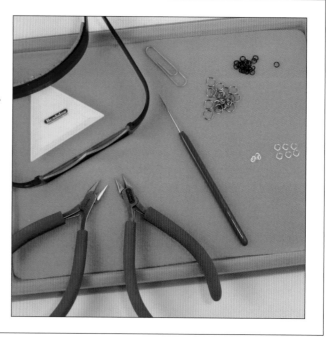

Chain Mail Weaves

For these introductory weaves, and any time you make chain mail, you will need two pairs of pliers in the combination that feels right for you. I have listed two different sizes and types of jump rings for each weave. To make the step-by-step photos, I used oversized rings in bright colors. I recommend that you use the same for practicing a weave. The second size mentioned is the size used to make the weave in a finished piece of jewelry.

The practice size jump rings will make the weave very loose and floppy. Don't concern yourself with this—I just want you to be able to see what you are doing and to be able to understand what you are learning. If you start by using the recommended jump ring sizes for the final piece, you may find them too small and get discouraged. I want you to have fun and enjoy your journey!

European 4-in-1

This is named the 4-in-1 because each jump ring in the center of the weave goes through the inside diameter of four other jump rings.

Length: 7½" (with extender)

WHAT YOU'LL NEED

practice jump rings
- **23** 16-gauge ⅜" (9.5mm) anodized aluminum jump rings in four colors (5 gold, 10 blue, 4 pink, and 4 turquoise)

finished piece
- **225** 18-gauge %₆₄" (3.57mm) jump rings
- lobster claw clasp

● **Preparation: Open the gold, pink, and turquoise jump rings. Close the blue jump rings.**

1. With an open gold jump ring, scoop up a paper clip and two closed blue jump rings. Close the gold jump ring. The paper clip acts as a handle.

2. Position the two closed blue jump rings from step 1 in such a way that you have "mouse ears" and a "forehead." Looking from left to right, the first blue jump ring is the mouse's left ear, the gold jump ring in the middle is the mouse's forehead, and the right blue jump ring is the mouse's right ear. If you flip the weave over, the mouse will not have a forehead.

3. Use an open gold jump ring to follow the path of the awl in photos 3a and 3b. **3a.** Entering from the front of the weave, go down through the mouse's right ear, around the back of the mouse's forehead,

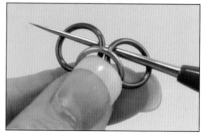

3b. and back up through the mouse's left ear from behind.

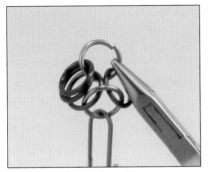

3c. Before closing the gold jump ring, add two closed blue jump rings. Close the gold jump ring.

4. Separate the blue rings. The bottoms of the newly added rings should overlap the tops of the blue rings in the first row.

Repeat steps 2 and 3 until you reach the desired length.

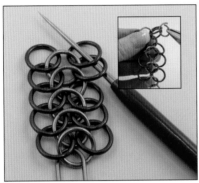

To widen the European 4-in-1

5. Start with the last two rows you just finished. Working down the right side of the weave and entering from the back, use an open pink jump ring to scoop up the second blue jump ring and the first blue jump ring (note the position of the awl). Close the pink jump ring.

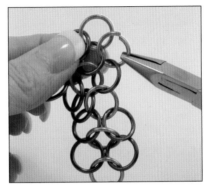

6. With an open pink jump ring and entering the weave from the back, pick up the third blue jump ring and the second blue jump ring. Close the pink jump ring.

7. Continue adding pink jump rings for the length of the weave.

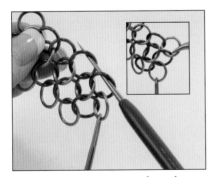

8. Flip the weave over. Start from the bottom and work your way up what was the left side and is now the right side of the weave. With an open turquoise jump ring entering from the front, scoop up the fifth blue jump ring and the fourth blue jump ring (note the position of the awl). Close the turquoise jump ring.

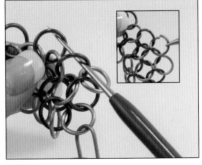

9. With an open turquoise jump ring entering from the front, pick up the fourth blue jump ring and the third blue jump ring. Close the turquoise jump ring.

10. Continue adding turquoise jump rings for the length of the weave.

Byzantine

For this weave, wherever you add one jump ring you must add another. This is called "doubling the ring." The rhythm of this weave is two rings, two rings, two rings, flip; two rings, two rings, two rings, flip. One unit of a Byzantine is a box, two rings, and a box. Byzantine units are used in a variety of weaves. Understanding the units of a weave is important when designing your own jewelry.

Length: 7¼"

WHAT YOU'LL NEED

practice jump rings
• **12** 16-gauge ⅜" (9.5mm) anodized aluminum jump rings in four colors (4 gold, 4 blue, 2 pink, and 2 turquoise)

finished piece
• **160** 18-gauge ⁹⁄₆₄" (3.57mm) jump rings
• lobster claw clasp

● **Preparation: Close two blue jump rings and open the rest.**

1. With an open gold jump ring, scoop up a paper clip and two closed blue jump rings.

2. Close the gold jump ring. Double the gold jump ring.

3. Hold the work by the paper clip. Fold down the two closed blue jump rings you added in step 1, one on either side of the paper clip.

4. Place one blue jump ring under your thumb and the other under your index finger. Push up the blue rings to create a hole for the next jump rings to pass through. This the "flip."

5. Rotate your hand so your thumb faces you. Spread the gold jump rings open. Use a beading awl to pick up the tops of the two blue jump rings.

6. Insert an open gold jump ring through the two blue jump rings. Close the gold jump ring. Double the gold jump ring.

7. Add two pink jump rings to the two gold jump rings added in step 6.

8. Add two turquoise jump rings to the two pink jump rings added in step 7.

9. Repeat steps 3–5 to create a path for the next two blue jump rings to go through.

10. With an open blue jump ring, pick up the two turquoise jump rings. Close the blue jump ring. Double the blue jump ring.

11. You now have completed one unit of the Byzantine weave. The two blue jump rings you added in step 10 are the first two jump rings in the pattern: two rings, two rings, two rings, flip. From this point in the weave, you will add two sets of two jump rings for a total of three sets of two jump rings; the third set you will flip. This is accomplished by repeating steps 7–10.

Byzantine creates a substantial rope-style chain, perfect for displaying charms or beads.

Möbius

In this weave, also known as a *rosette*, each new jump ring is added through all of the previous jump rings and snugged up next to the previous ring. I'm demonstrating a four-ring Möbius (mœ-bē-əs), but feel free to add as many rings to yours as you can fit (the finished earrings have six).

WHAT YOU'LL NEED

practice jump rings
- **4** 16-gauge ⅜" (9.5mm) anodized aluminum jump rings in four colors (orange, turquoise, blue, and pink)

finished piece
- **12** 18-gauge ¹⁵⁄₆₄" (5.95mm) jump rings
- **2** 18-gauge ⅛" (3.18mm) jump rings
- **2** 18-gauge ⁵⁄₃₂"(3.97mm) jump rings
- pair of earring wires

● **Preparation: Open the orange, blue, and pink jump rings and close the turquoise jump rings.**

1. Scoop up a closed turquoise jump ring with an open gold jump ring. Close the gold jump ring.

2. Scoop up the gold and the turquoise jump rings with an open purple jump ring. Close the purple jump ring.

3. Situate the purple jump ring so that it nestles inside the gold and turquoise jump rings.

4. With an open pink jump ring scoop up the gold, turquoise, and purple jump rings. Situate the three jump rings so that they nestle inside each other. In order for the weave to lie correctly you must nestle the jump rings prior to adding any additional jump rings.

5. At this point you can continue to add jump rings until desired effect is achieved. This picture depicts a four ring unit of Möbius. As you will see in the projects, a Möbius unit can be connected using other jump rings.

Spiral

The Spiral weave twists around like a staircase. Here, you'll learn the two-jump-ring Spiral weave, although you can make a Spiral weave with more than two jump rings.

Length: 7½" (with extender)

WHAT YOU'LL NEED

practice jump rings
- **10** 16-gauge ⅜"(9.5mm) jump rings in four colors (4 blue, 2 pink, 2 yellow, and 2 turquoise)

finished piece
- **137** 20-gauge ¹¹⁄₆₄" (4.37mm) jump rings
- **9** 20 gauge ⁹⁄₆₄" (3.57mm) jump rings
- lobster claw clasp

● **Preparation: Close two blue jump rings and open the rest.**

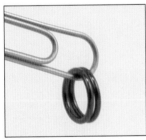

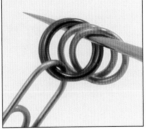

1. Add two closed blue jump rings to a paper clip.

2. With an open pink jump ring, scoop up the two blue jump rings. Close the pink jump ring. Double the pink jump ring.

3. With an open yellow jump ring, scoop up the two pink jump rings and the two blue jump rings (path shown with the awl). Close the yellow jump ring. Double the yellow jump ring.

TIP

For this weave, you only pick up the two previous sets of jump rings added.

4. With an open turquoise jump ring, scoop up the pink and the yellow jump rings. Close the turquoise jump ring. Double the turquoise jump ring.

5. With a blue jump ring, scoop up the two yellow jump rings and the two turquoise jump rings. Close the blue jump ring. Double the blue jump ring.

6. The chain is beginning to twist. When you use smaller jump rings the twist is more pronounced. Repeat step 5 for the desired length.

Japanese

Length: 7"

WHAT YOU'LL NEED

practice jump rings
- **14** 16-gauge ⅜" (9.5mm) jump rings (large) in two colors (pink and turquoise)
- **24** 18-gauge ³⁄₁₆" (4.76mm) anodized aluminum jump rings (small) in two colors (green and purple).

finished piece
- **135** 20-gauge ⁷⁄₆₄" (2.78mm) (small) jump rings
- **73** 18-gauge ¹¹⁄₆₄" (4.37mm) (large) jump rings

The Japanese weaves consist of horizontal jump rings going through vertical jump rings. Use the same size jump rings, or add contrast with two different sizes. I will be demonstrating both with the projects on pages 32, 46, and 50.

We'll use large and small jump rings in the Japanese 12-in-2 pattern to make a simple flower pattern. The size jump rings you will need for this project are 18-gauge ¹¹⁄₆₄" for the large jump rings and 20-gauge ⁷⁄₆₄" for the small jump rings. The pink ring becomes the center of the diamond-shaped component.

● **Preparation: Open all the large rings and close all the small rings.**

1. With an open large pink jump ring, scoop up 12 small closed green jump rings. Close the large pink jump ring.

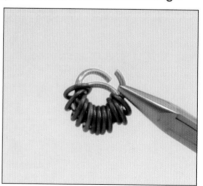

2. Double the large pink jump ring. Take care not to cross the two large pink jump rings.

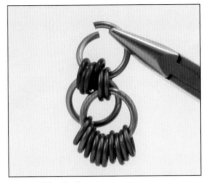

3. With an open large turquoise jump rings, scoop up any two small green jump rings. Before closing the large turquoise jump ring, add four small closed purple jump rings. Close the large turquoise jump ring.

4. Double the large turquoise jump ring.

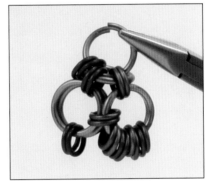

5. With an open large turquoise jump ring, scoop up the next two small green jump rings and two of the four small purple jump rings added in step 3. Add two closed small purple jump rings. Close the large turquoise jump ring.

6. Double the large turquoise jump ring.

7. With an open large turquoise jump ring, scoop up the next two small green jump rings and the two small purple jump rings added in step 5 . Before closing the large turquoise jump ring, add two small closed purple jump rings. Close the large turquoise jump ring.

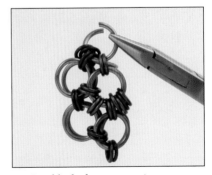

8. Double the large turquoise jump ring.

9. With an open large turquoise jump ring, scoop up the next two small green jump rings and the two small purple jump rings added in step 7. Before closing the large turquoise jump ring, add two small closed purple jump rings. Close the large turquoise jump ring.

10. Double the large turquoise jump ring.

11. With an open large turquoise jump ring, scoop up the next two small green jump rings and the two small purple jump rings added in step 9. Before closing the large turquoise jump ring, add two small closed purple jump rings. Close the large turquoise jump ring.

12. Double the large turquoise jump ring.

13. With an open large turquoise jump ring, scoop up the other two small purple jump rings added in step 3, the last two small green jump rings, and the two small purple jump rings added in step 11. Close the jump ring.

14. Double the large turquoise jump ring. You have completed one component.

Shaggy Loop

I love making jewelry using the Shaggy Loop weave pattern. The weave is very versatile and can be added to other weaves to enhance their appearance. In these earrings, I've combined Shaggy Loop and Byzantine.

Length: 2¼"

WHAT YOU'LL NEED

practice jump rings
- **9** 16-gauge ⅜" (9.5mm) anodized aluminum jump rings in four colors (2 pink, 4 gold, 1 purple, 2 turquoise)

finished piece
- **186** 18-gauge ⅛" (3.18mm) sterling silver jump rings
- **2** 3-1 connectors
- pair of earring wires

● **Preparation: Open all pink and purple rings and close all gold and turquoise rings.**

1. With an open pink jump ring, scoop up a paper clip and two closed gold jump rings. Close the pink jump ring.

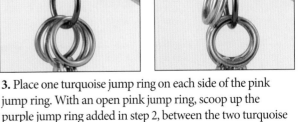

2. Place one gold jump ring on each side of the paper clip. With an open purple jump ring, scoop up the pink jump ring added in step 1, between the two gold jump rings. Before closing the purple jump ring, add two closed turquoise jump rings. Close the purple jump ring.

3. Place one turquoise jump ring on each side of the pink jump ring. With an open pink jump ring, scoop up the purple jump ring added in step 2, between the two turquoise jump rings. Before closing the pink jump ring, add two closed gold jump rings. Close the pink jump ring. Repeat for the desired length.

Parallel or Helm's

Like the Japanese weave, the Parallel or the Helm's weave uses two different sizes of jump rings. This weave also introduces the *orbiting jump ring* concept. An orbiting jump ring does not go through any other jump rings. Think of it as a jump ring that is "sandwiched" between other jump rings.

● **Preparation: Open four pink, two yellow, and two purple jump rings and close the remaining two purple rings.**

1. With a large open pink jump ring, scoop up a paper clip and two small closed purple jump rings. Close the pink jump ring.

2. Double the large pink jump ring.

3. With a large open yellow jump ring encircle or *orbit* around the two small purple jump rings by going between the two large pink jump rings and around the two small purple jump rings. Do not go through either of the large pink jump rings or through the two small purple jump rings. The yellow jump ring is an orbiting ring, meaning it does not go through any other jump rings. Close the large yellow jump ring.

4. With an open large pink jump ring, go through the two small purple jump rings, taking care not to go through any other jump rings. Close the large pink jump ring.

5. Flip the weave over and with an open large pink jump ring, go through the two small purple jump rings, for a pink jump ring on each side of the yellow jump ring added in step 3. Close the large pink jump ring.

6. With an open small purple jump ring, scoop up the two large pink jump rings added in steps 4 and 5. Close the small purple jump ring.

7. Double the small purple jump ring.

8. Repeat step 3 with an open large yellow jump ring.

9. Repeat steps 4–8 for the desired length.

Projects

PROJECT 1
3-in-3 Chain Necklace & Earrings

Length: 22½"

WHAT YOU'LL NEED

Necklace
- **156** 19-gauge ³⁄₁₆" enameled (silvered) copper jump rings, lime
- **156** 19-gauge ³⁄₁₆" enameled (silvered) copper jump rings, peacock blue
- **156** 19-gauge ³⁄₁₆" enameled (silvered) copper jump rings, peach

Earrings
- **18** 19-gauge ³⁄₁₆" enameled (silvered) copper jump rings, lime
- **18** 19-gauge ³⁄₁₆" enameled (silvered) copper jump rings, peacock blue
- **12** 19-gauge ³⁄₁₆" enameled (silvered) copper jump rings, peach
- pair enameled (silvered) copper earring wires, peach

This is a fabulous weave to start your journey into the ancient art of chain mail. The weave is three jump rings connected to three jump rings connected to three jump rings…well, you get the idea! This necklace reminds me of when I was little girl in school. We made a chain out of different colored construction paper strips. Each student made a section and then the teacher took the chain and hung it on the wall all around the classroom. This weave is simple, but it can also be elegant.

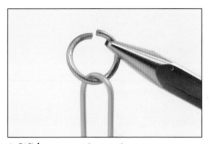

1. With an open jump ring, scoop up a paper clip. Close the jump ring.

2. Repeat step 1 twice for a total of three jump rings.

3. With an open jump ring in a new color, scoop up all three jump rings added in steps 1 and 2, and close the jump ring.

4. Repeat step 3 twice for a total of three jump rings.

5. Keep adding jump rings in this three-ring pattern until the necklace is the desired length. (Note that this necklace has no clasp, so make sure it fits over your head.)

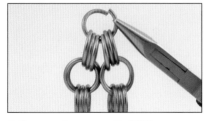

6. Remove the paper clip. With an open jump ring, scoop up each end of the necklace and close the jump ring. Repeat twice for a total of three jump rings.

Make earrings with eight sets of links.

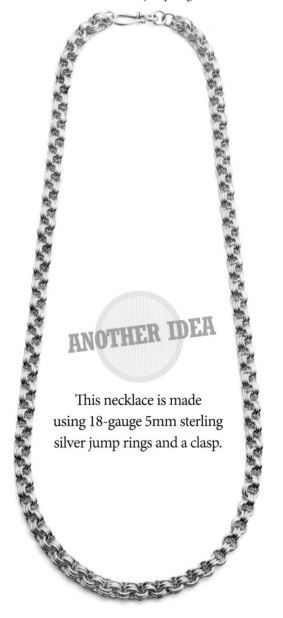

ANOTHER IDEA

This necklace is made using 18-gauge 5mm sterling silver jump rings and a clasp.

PROJECT2
Shaggy Loop Earrings

This weave is versatile and easy to do. The "shaggy loops" can be plain jump rings, or you can add accent beads or drops to them.

Finished length: 1¼"

WHAT YOU'LL NEED

- **34** 21-gauge ⁵⁄₃₂" jump rings, sterling silver
- **18** Swarovski drops, amethyst
- pair of earring wires, sterling silver

● Preparation: Open 26 jump rings and close eight jump rings.

1. With an open jump ring, scoop up an amethyst drop. Close the jump ring. Repeat 14 times to make a total of 16 drop components.

2. With an open jump ring, scoop up an earring wire, an amethyst component, a closed jump ring, and an amethyst component. Close the jump ring.

3. Slide the components to either side of the earring wire. With an open jump ring, scoop up the closed jump ring added in step 2.

4. Add an amethyst component, a closed jump ring, and an amethyst component. Close the jump ring.

5. Slide the components to either side. With an open jump ring, scoop up the closed jump ring added in step 4.

6. Add an amethyst component, a closed jump ring, and an amethyst component. Close the jump ring.

7. With an open jump ring, scoop up [the closed] jump ring added in step 6. [Add an ame]thyst component, a closed [jump ring, an]d an amethyst component. [Close the jum]p ring.

8. With an open jump ring, scoop up the closed jump ring added in step 7. Add an amethyst drop. Close the jump ring.

9. Make a second earring.

ANOTHER IDEA

Instead of adding an amethyst drop to the jump rings as in step 1, add 3.4mm drop beads and a clasp for a bracelet.

PROJECT3
Stitch Marker Set

These stitch markers are so easy to make for the knitters in your life! I use lightweight jump rings that are either enamel-coated copper or anodized aluminum, but choose any type of material you like. Be sure to close the jump rings completely so they won't snag the yarn. For help in making a Möbius, refer to Chain Mail Weaves (p. 22).

WHAT YOU'LL NEED

Large markers (for six markers)
- **6** 18-gauge ½" enamel coated copper jump rings in various colors
- **36** 19-gauge ³⁄₁₆" enamel-coated copper jump rings in various colors

Small markers (for six markers)
- **6** 16-gauge ³⁄₈" anodized aluminum jump rings in various colors
- **30** 18-gauge ⁹⁄₆₄" enamel coated copper jump rings in various colors

These five small stitch markers (left) have a five-ring Möbius embellishment. The six large stitch markers (below) have a six-ring Möbius decoration.

Large Stitch Markers

● **Preparation (for each stitch marker): Open five 19-gauge ³⁄₁₆" jump rings, close one 19-gauge ³⁄₁₆" jump ring, and close one 18-gauge ½" jump ring.**

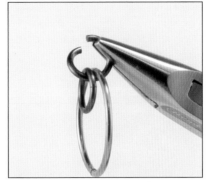

1. With an open 19-gauge ³⁄₁₆" jump ring, scoop up a closed 18-gauge ½" jump ring and a closed 19-gauge ³⁄₁₆" jump ring. Close the jump ring.

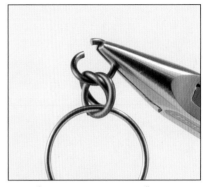

2. With an open 19-gauge ³⁄₁₆" jump ring, scoop up the two 19-gauge ³⁄₁₆" jump rings added in step 1. Close the jump ring.

3. With an open 19-gauge ³⁄₁₆" jump ring, scoop through all three of the 19-gauge ³⁄₁₆" jump rings in the same order to create the cluster. Close the jump ring.

4. With an open 19-gauge ³⁄₁₆" jump ring, scoop through all four of the 19-gauge ³⁄₁₆" jump rings in the same order. Close the jump ring.

5. With an open 19-gauge ³⁄₁₆" jump ring, scoop through all five ofthe 19-gauge ³⁄₁₆" jump rings in the same order. Close the jump ring.

6. Repeat steps 1–5 to make additional large stitch markers.

TIP

When making the six-ring Möbius, make sure all of the jump rings are lying in the same direction and snuggled against each other. If one looks wonky, flip it to fit better.

TIP

The nesting of the jump rings in this Möbius is incorrect. The purple and the turquoise jump rings are correct but the gold jump ring is lying in the wrong direction. If you flip the gold jump ring toward you, it will nestle correctly.

Small stitch markers

Preparation (for each stitch marker): Close one 16-gauge ⅜" jump ring, close one 18-gauge ⁹⁄₆₄" jump ring, and open four 18-gauge ⁹⁄₆₄" jump rings.

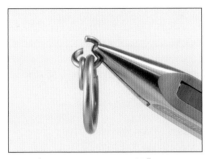

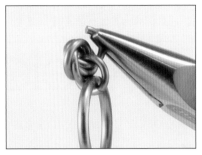

1. With an open 18-gauge ⁹⁄₆₄" jump ring, scoop up the closed 16-gauge ⅜" jump ring and a closed 18-gauge ⁹⁄₆₄" jump ring. Close the jump ring.

2. With an open 18-gauge ⁹⁄₆₄" jump ring, scoop up the two 18-gauge ⁹⁄₆₄" jump rings added in step 1. Close the jump ring.

3. With an open 18-gauge ⁹⁄₆₄" jump ring, scoop through all three 18-gauge ⁹⁄₆₄" jump rings in the same order. Close the jump ring.

4. With an open 18-gauge ⁹⁄₆₄" jump ring, scoop up the four 18-gauge ⁹⁄₆₄" jump rings in the same order. Close the jump ring.

5. Repeat steps 1–4 to make additional small stitch markers.

TIP You can make all the Möbius units first, and then use a small jump ring to connect each to a large jump ring.

PROJECT4
Crystal Parallel Bracelet

The sparkle in this bracelet is amazing. The crystals add a whole new dimension to the Parallel weave. Don't be afraid to use sterling silver jump rings with gold-filled jump rings. It's OK to mix metals.

Finished length: 7"

WHAT YOU'LL NEED

- **34** 18-gauge 9⁄64" jump rings, sterling silver
- **50** 18-gauge 15⁄64" jump rings, sterling silver
- **2** 20-gauge 1⁄8" jump rings, sterling silver
- **16** 4mm bicone crystals
- **2** loop crimps
- flexible beading wire, .019
- clasp, sterling silver

1. With an open 20-gauge ⅛" jump ring, scoop up the clasp. Close the jump ring.

2. With an open 18-gauge ¹⁵⁄₆₄" jump ring, scoop up the 20-gauge ⅛" jump ring added in step 1 and two closed 18-gauge ⁹⁄₆₄" jump rings. Close the jump ring. Double the 18-gauge ¹⁵⁄₆₄" jump ring.

3. Continue with Parallel Weave following the instructions in Chain Mail Weaves (p. 28) using the 18-gauge ¹⁵⁄₆₄" jump rings as the large jump rings and the 18-gauge ⁹⁄₆₄" jump rings as the small jump rings. Make the bracelet ½" larger than the desired size. The crystals will take up the extra length.

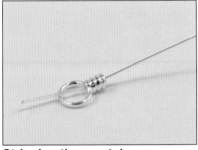

Stringing the crystals
4. String the beading wire through the hole in the loop crimp. Extend the wire past the loop. This will help when you crimp because you will hold onto the large ring of the crimp and the excess wire.

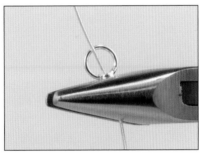

5. With chainnose pliers, grasp the crimp right below the loop and squeeze the crimp to the beading wire. Crimp using the back portion of the pliers, not the tips.

6. Trim the wire tail.

7. Open the 20-gauge ⅛" jump ring attached to the clasp, flip down one of the 18-gauge ¹⁵⁄₆₄" jump rings, place the loop crimp onto the 20-gauge ⅛" jump ring, reattach the 18-gauge ¹⁵⁄₆₄" jump ring to the 20-gauge ⅛" jump ring, and close the 20-gauge ⅛" jump ring. The loop crimp should be between the two 18-gauge ⁹⁄₆₄" jump rings.

8. String the beading wire over the 18-gauge $^{15}/_{64}$" floating jump ring, under the 18-gauge $^{15}/_{64}$" jump ring, between the two 18-gauge $^{9}/_{64}$" jump rings, and over the floating 18-gauge $^{15}/_{64}$" jump ring. The side view is of a piece of wire illustrating the path of the beading wire.

9. String a crystal on the beading wire.

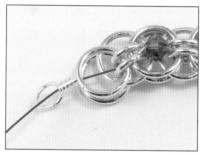

10. Repeat steps 8 and 9 until the end of the beading wire is on top of the last 18-gauge $^{15}/_{64}$" floating jump ring and between the last two 18-gauge $^{15}/_{64}$" jump rings.

11. String the second loop crimp on the end of the beading wire. Make sure that the bracelet fits around your wrist. Flatten the crimp.

12. With an open 20-gauge $^{1}/_{8}$" jump ring, scoop up a 18-gauge $^{15}/_{64}$" jump ring, the loop crimp, the other 18-gauge $^{15}/_{64}$" jump ring, and the remaining clasp half. Close the 20-gauge $^{1}/_{8}$" jump ring.

TIP
Before adding the final loop crimp place a bead stopper on the wire and check the fit of the bracelet. Mark the wire with a permanent marker so you know where to place the final loop crimp.

PROJECT5
Wedding Knot Bracelet

Finished length: 6¾"

WHAT YOU'LL NEED

- **216** 20-gauge ³⁄₁₆" jump rings, silver-plated
- **123** 20-gauge ⅛" jump rings, silver-plated
- 3-strand slide clasp, silver-plated

This lovely bracelet is a combination of two techniques: the Japanese weave and the Möbius weave. For additional instructions, see Chain Mail Weaves (Japanese, p. 24, and Möbius, p. 22). The Möbius pattern adds texture and interest to this bracelet. The angles of the rings also catch the light.

● **Preparation: Open all of the jump rings.**

1. With an open 20-gauge ⅛" jump ring, scoop up a clasp loop. Close the jump ring.

2. With an open 20-gauge ³⁄₁₆" jump ring, scoop up the 20-gauge ⅛" jump ring added in step 1. Close the jump ring.

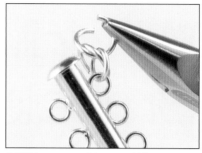

3. With an open 20-gauge ³⁄₁₆" jump ring, scoop up the 20-gauge ⅛" jump ring added in step 1 and go through the 20-gauge ³⁄₁₆" jump ring added in step 2 to form the beginning of a three-ring Möbius. Close the jump ring.

4. Repeat step 3 and go through both 20-gauge ³⁄₁₆" jump rings added in steps 2 and 3. Close the jump ring. You have now completed the three-ring Möbius.

5. With an open 20-gauge ⅛" jump ring, scoop up the completed Möbius from step 4. Close the jump ring.

6. With an open 20-gauge ³⁄₁₆" jump ring, scoop up the 20-gauge ⅛" jump ring added in step 5. Close the jump ring.

7. With an open 20-gauge ³⁄₁₆" jump ring, scoop up the 20-gauge ⅛" jump ring added in step 5 and go through the 20-gauge ³⁄₁₆" jump ring from step 6. Close the jump ring.

8. With an open 20-gauge ³⁄₁₆" jump ring, scoop up the 20-gauge ⅛" jump ring added in step 5 and go through both 20-gauge ³⁄₁₆" jump rings from steps 6 and 7. Close the jump ring.

9. Repeat steps 5–8 22 more times.

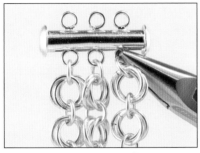

10. Repeat steps 1–9 twice, beginning each new row with a remaining clasp loop.

11. With an open 20-gauge ⅛" jump ring, link the first Möbius in the first row and the first Möbius in the second row. Close the jump ring.

12. Continue linking the Möbius in the first and second rows together.

13 Repeat steps 11 and 12 to link the Möbius in the second and third rows.

14. With an open 20-gauge ⅛" jump ring, link the last Möbius to a clasp loop. Close the jump ring. Repeat with the remaining rows.

ANOTHER IDEA

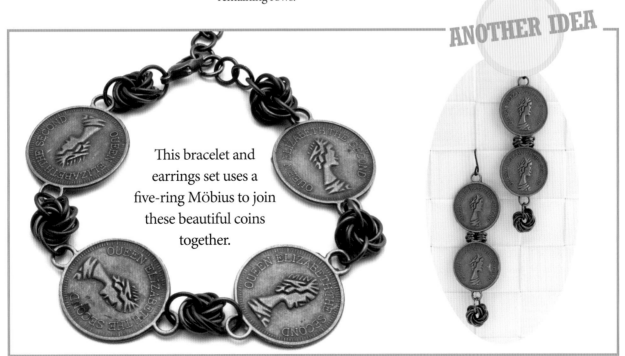

This bracelet and earrings set uses a five-ring Möbius to join these beautiful coins together.

PROJECT6
Twisted Rhinestone Bracelet

Finished length: 6¾"

WHAT YOU'LL NEED

- **152** 20-gauge ⁷⁄₆₄" jump rings, silver-plated
- **84** 18-gauge ¹¹⁄₆₄" jump rings, brass
- 2½" rhinestone connector twist, crystal
- 3-strand slide clasp, brass

The Czech rhinestone connector I used for this bracelet is normally used as a connector for lingerie, but by thinking outside of the box, I was able to use it for this bracelet. Don't be afraid to look at components and figure out a way to use them with your chain mail.

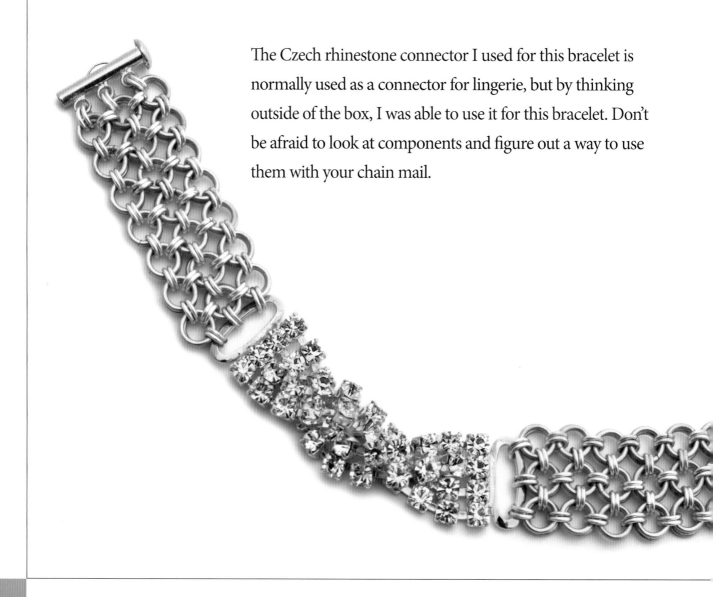

● Open 24 20-gauge ⁷⁄₆₄" silver jump rings. Close all remaining 20-gauge ⁷⁄₆₄" silver jump rings. Open all of the 18-gauge ¹¹⁄₆₄" brass jump rings.

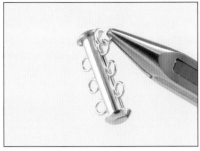

1. With an open 20-gauge ⁷⁄₆₄" silver jump ring, scoop up a clasp loop. Close the jump ring.

2. Double the silver jump ring.

3. Repeat steps 1 and 2 for the remaining clasp loops to have two silver jump rings in each of the three clasp loops.

4. Repeat steps 1 and 2 on the other side of the clasp.

5. Repeat step 3.

6. With an open 18-gauge ¹¹⁄₆₄" brass jump ring, scoop up two of the 20-gauge ⁷⁄₆₄" silver jump rings on one end of the clasp and add four closed 20-gauge ⁷⁄₆₄" silver jump rings. Close the brass jump ring.

7. Double the brass jump ring.

8. With an open brass jump ring, scoop up the two middle silver jump rings from the clasp and two of the four closed silver jump rings added in step 6, and add four more closed silver jump rings. Close the brass jump ring.

9. Double the brass jump ring.

10. With an open brass jump ring, scoop up the remaining two silver jump rings on the working side of the clasp and two of the four jump rings added in step 8, and add two closed silver jump rings. Close the brass jump ring.

11. Double the brass jump ring.

12. With an open brass jump ring, scoop up the two closed silver jump rings added in step 10 and add four closed silver jump rings.

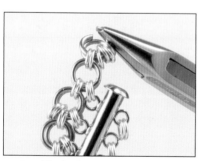

13. Double the brass jump ring.

ANOTHER IDEA

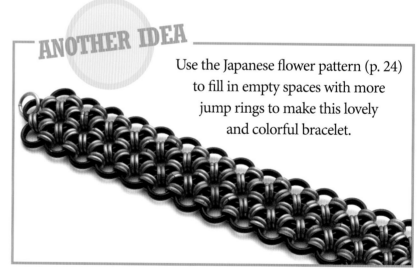

Use the Japanese flower pattern (p. 24) to fill in empty spaces with more jump rings to make this lovely and colorful bracelet.

14. With an open brass jump ring, scoop up two of the closed silver rings added in step 12 and two of the closed silver jump rings added in step 8, and add four closed silver jump rings. Close the brass jump ring.

15. Double the brass jump ring.

16. With an open brass jump ring, scoop up two of the silver jump rings added in step 14 and two of the silver jump rings added in step 6, and add two closed silver jump rings. Close the brass jump ring.

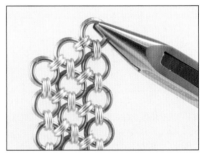

17. Double the brass jump ring.

18. Repeat steps 12–17 four more times.

19. Repeat steps 12–17, but do not add any additional silver jump rings.

20. With an open silver jump ring, scoop up one set of brass jump rings and one end of the connector. Close the silver jump ring. If you prefer, you can substitute 20-gauge ⅛" jump rings here to attach the connector. They are a bit larger and easier to close.

21. Double the silver jump ring.

22. Repeat steps 20 and 21 twice to connect the remaining sets of two brass jump rings.

23. Repeat steps 1–22 using the remaining clasp half and the other side of the connector.

PROJECT7
Rhinestone Hand Flower

I bet you never thought that such a lovely hand flower could be made using a fancy lingerie connector! When I found the connector, I knew I had to incorporate it into my chain mail. Because it has three connectors, it's perfect for a hand flower. Don't be afraid to experiment with objects not originally designed for jewelry. You'll be surprised how creative you can be!

Finished length: 8"

WHAT YOU'LL NEED

- Czech rhinestone connector 3-way flower crystal
- **32** 18-gauge ¹⁵⁄₆₄" jump rings, sterling silver
- **96** 18-gauge ⅛" jump rings, sterling silver
- **16** 18 ⁹⁄₆₄" jump rings, sterling silver
- **26** clear/transparent 4.8-5mm silicone rings

● Preparation: Open all of the 18-gauge $^{15}/_{64}$" jump rings and all of the 18-gauge $^{9}/_{64}$" jump rings. Open 36 18-gauge $^{1}/_{8}$" jump rings and close 60 18-gauge $^{1}/_{8}$" jump rings.

1. Add four 18-gauge $^{1}/_{8}$" jump rings to each end of the 3-way connector.

2. With an open 18-gauge $^{15}/_{64}$" jump ring, scoop up the four 18-gauge $^{1}/_{8}$" jump rings on the center rhinestone chain of the connector and add six closed 18-gauge $^{1}/_{8}$" jump rings. Close the jump ring.

3. Double the 18-gauge $^{15}/_{64}$" jump ring.

4. With an open 18-gauge $^{15}/_{64}$" jump ring, scoop up two middle 18-gauge $^{1}/_{8}$" jump rings added in step 2 and add six 18-gauge $^{1}/_{8}$" closed jump rings. Close the jump ring.

5. Double the 18-gauge $^{15}/_{64}$" jump ring.

6. Working from the left side, with an open 18-gauge $^{9}/_{64}$" jump ring, scoop up two of the 18-gauge $^{1}/_{8}$" jump rings added in step 2 and two of the 18-gauge $^{1}/_{8}$" jump rings added in step 4. Close the jump ring.

7. Double the 18-gauge $^{9}/_{64}$" jump ring.

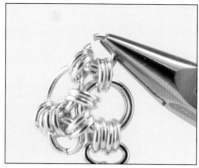

8. Working from the right side, with the open 18-gauge ⁹⁄₆₄" jump ring, scoop up two of the 18-gauge ⅛" jump rings added in step 2 and two of the 18-gauge ⅛" jump rings added in step 4. Close the jump ring.

9. Double the 18-gauge ⁹⁄₆₄" jump ring.

10. With an open 18-gauge ¹⁵⁄₆₄" jump ring, scoop up the two remaining 18-gauge ⅛" jump rings from the six 18-gauge ⅛" jump rings added in step 4 and add six closed 18-gauge ⅛" jump rings. Close the jump ring.

11. Double the 18-gauge ¹⁵⁄₆₄" jump ring.

12. Repeat steps 4–9.

13. With an open 18-gauge ¹⁵⁄₆₄" jump ring, scoop up the two remaining 18-gauge ⅛" jump rings from the six 18-gauge ⅛" jump rings last added. Before closing, add four closed 18-gauge ⅛" jump rings. Close the jump ring. Double the 18-gauge ¹⁵⁄₆₄" jump ring.

14. With an open 18-gauge ⅛" jump ring, scoop up two of the closed 18-gauge ⅛" jump rings added in step 13 and two 18-gauge ⅛" jump rings. Close the jump ring. Double the 18-gauge ⅛" jump ring.

15. With an open 18-gauge ⅛" jump ring, scoop up two of the closed 18-gauge ⅛" jump rings added in step 14 and two 18-gauge ⅛" jump rings. Close the jump ring. Double the 18-gauge ⅛" jump ring.

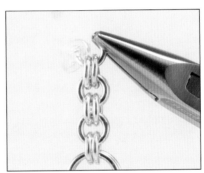

16. With an open 18-gauge ⅛" jump ring, scoop up the two closed 18-gauge ⅛" jump rings added in step 14 and two silicone rings. Close the jump ring. Double the jump ring.

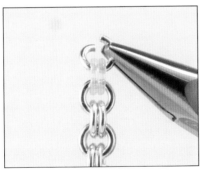
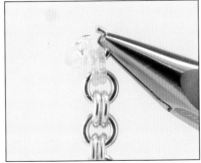

17. With an open 18-gauge ⅛" jump ring, scoop up the two silicone rings added in step 16 and two silicone rings. Close the jump ring. Double the jump ring.

18. Repeat step 17 five more times.

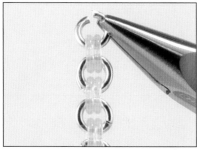 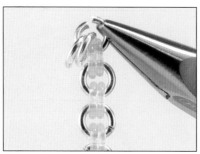

19. With an open 18-gauge ⅛" jump ring, scoop up the two silicone rings added in the last step and add two closed 18-gauge ⅛" jump rings. Close the jump ring. Double the jump ring.

 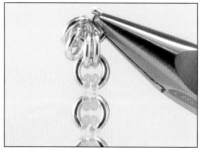 

20. With an open 18-gauge ⅛" jump ring, scoop up the two 18-gauge ⅛" jump rings added in step 19 and two closed 18-gauge ⅛" jump rings. Close the jump ring. Double the jump ring.

21. With an open 18-gauge ⅛" jump ring, scoop up the two 18-gauge ⅛" jump rings added in step 20 and the two 18-gauge ⅛" jump rings left from step 13. Close the jump ring. Double the jump ring.

This completes the portion of the hand flower that goes around your finger. Now you will complete the portion that goes around your wrist.

23. Starting with the remaining rhinestone chain, repeat steps 2–9.

22. Starting with either end of the remaining two rhinestone chains, repeat steps 2–9.

TIP

Check the fit around your finger and wrist. If necessary, add or subtract silicone rings to adjust the fit.

24. With an open 18-gauge ¹⁵⁄₆₄" jump ring, scoop up the two remaining 18-gauge ⅛" jump rings from the six 18-gauge ⅛" jump rings added in step 23, and add two silicone rings. Close the jump ring. Double the jump ring.

25. With an open 18-gauge ¹⁵⁄₆₄" jump ring, scoop up the two silicone rings added in step 24 and add two silicone rings. Close the jump ring. Double the jump ring.

26. Repeat step 25 four more times.

27. With an open 18-gauge ¹⁵⁄₆₄" jump ring, scoop up the two silicone rings added in step 26 and the last two 18-gauge ⅛" jump rings added in step 22. Close the jump ring. Double the jump ring.

PROJECT8

Sideways Euro 4-in-1 Bracelet

Finished length: 8"

WHAT YOU'LL NEED

- **125** 18-gauge ⁹⁄₆₄" jump rings, purple
- **124** 18-gauge ⁹⁄₆₄" jump rings, turquoise
- 2-strand clasp, silver-plated

This bracelet drapes like fabric. You will love the liquid fluidity of this smooth and supple weave. Turning the European 4-in-1 weave sideways adds a different texture and feel.

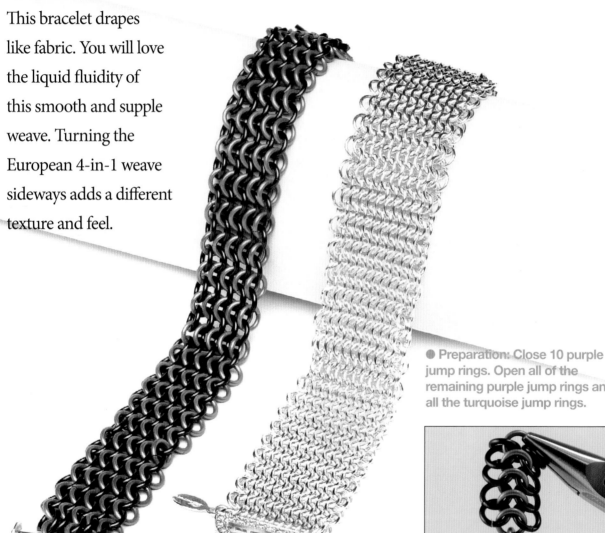

● Preparation: Close 10 purple jump rings. Open all of the remaining purple jump rings and all the turquoise jump rings.

1. Make a strip of European 4-in-1 using the Chain Mail Weaves (p. 18) instructions. Use the purple jump rings for the ears and the turquoise jump rings for the forehead. The strip should have five sets of ears.

2. With an open turquoise jump ring, scoop up the second and first ear on the right side. Close the turquoise jump ring. (For further clarification, refer to European 4-in-1 step 5.)

3. With an open turquoise jump ring, scoop up the third and the second ear on the right side. Close the turquoise jump ring. (For further clarification, refer to European 4-in-1 step 6.)

4. With an open turquoise jump ring, scoop up the fourth and third ear on the right side. Close the turquoise jump ring.

5. With an open turquoise jump ring, scoop up the fifth and fourth ear on the right side. Close the turquoise jump ring.

6. In order to keep this bracelet from tapering, you will need to add one more turquoise jump ring to the bottom purple jump ring. With an open turquoise jump ring, scoop up the fifth ear on the right side. Close the turquoise jump ring. This jump ring will stack on top of the previous turquoise jump ring.

7. All of the turquoise jump rings will stack on top of the previous turquoise jump rings.

8. Starting at the bottom right of the weave, with an open purple jump ring, scoop up the single turquoise jump ring added in step 6 and the turquoise jump ring added in step 5. Close the purple jump ring.

9. With an open purple jump ring, scoop up the turquoise jump ring added in step 5 and the turquoise jump added in step 4. Close the purple jump ring.

10. With an open purple jump ring, scoop up the turquoise jump ring added in step 4 and the turquoise jump added in step 3. Close the purple jump ring.

11. With an open purple jump ring, scoop up the turquoise jump ring added in step 3 and the turquoise jump added in step 2. Close the purple jump ring.

12. With an open purple jump ring, scoop up the turquoise jump ring added in step 2. Close the purple jump ring.

13. Repeat steps 1–12 until you reach the desired length of the bracelet.

14. Attach the clasp to each end of the bracelet.

ANOTHER IDEA

To make a simple pair of earrings, repeat step 1. Repeat steps 2–5 until you have tapered down to one jump ring. Repeat steps 2–5 on the second half of the weave, again tapering down to one jump ring. Connect the last single jump ring to an earring wire.

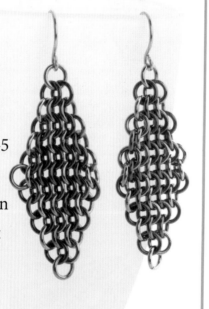

PROJECT 9
Butterfly Earrings

The beauty of these earrings is in their simplicity. Interlocking the jump rings in this pattern makes an airy, open weave. By joining the two sections, you create what appears to be a butterfly.

Finished length: 1¼"

WHAT YOU'LL NEED

- **56** 18-gauge ³⁄₁₆" artistic wire chain mail jump rings, copper
- pair of earring wires, copper

● **Preparation: Close eight jump rings and open 48 jump rings.**

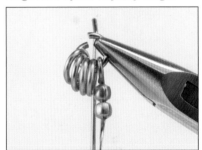

1. With an open jump ring, scoop up one earring wire and four closed jump rings. Close the jump ring.

2. With an open jump ring, scoop up the first two jump rings of the four added in step 1. Close the jump ring.

3. With an open jump ring, scoop up the last two jump rings of the four added in step 1. Close the jump ring.

4. With an open jump ring, scoop up the two center jump rings added in step 1. Close the jump ring.

5. Double the ring. Be sure to sandwich the added rings from steps 2 and 3.

6. With an open jump ring, scoop up the left single jump ring added in step 2. Close the jump ring.

  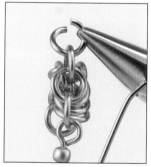

7. With an open jump ring, go through the center jump rings added in steps 4 and 5, and the left jump ring added in step 2. Close the jump ring.

8. With an open jump ring, go through the center jump rings added in steps 4 and 5, and the right jump ring added in step 3. Close the jump ring.

9. With an open jump ring, go through the right single jump ring added in step 3. Close the jump ring.

10. Working from the paper clip or a twist tie handle, repeat steps 1–9. Remove the paper clip or the twist tie.

11. With an open jump ring, connect the two sections by scooping up all four jump rings added in steps 6–9 on each piece. Close the jump ring.

ANOTHER IDEA

Make a bracelet by making additional sections following steps 1–9 and joining them together following step 11. Complete with a clasp.

PROJECT 10
Leather & Lace Bracelet

I have always loved the smell and feel of leather. I also love mixing leather with chain mail because it gives an industrial feel. This bracelet is easy to make if you start with a pre-punched leather blank. If you can't find a pre-punched blank, use an awl or hole-punching pliers to create the foundation on a plain leather bracelet.

Finished length: 8½"

WHAT YOU'LL NEED

- Leather bracelet blank with 35 holes
- **33** 20-gauge ³⁄₁₆" jump rings, silver-plated
- **31** 18-gauge ¹⁵⁄₆₄" jump rings, silver-plated
- **90** 20-gauge ³⁄₃₂" jump rings, silver-plated
- beading awl or hole-punching pliers (optional)

● Preparation: Open all of the 20-gauge ³⁄₁₆" and 18-gauge ¹⁵⁄₆₄" jump rings. Close all of the 20-gauge ³⁄₃₂" jump rings.

NOTE: In some cases, the holes on the bracelet blank will need to be made a bit larger. I use a beading awl with a tapered point. Don't worry if you make the hole too large; it will self-mend.

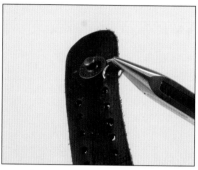 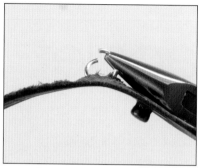 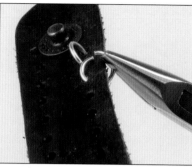

1. With an open 20-gauge ³⁄₁₆" jump ring, come up from the back of the bracelet through the first hole and go down through the second hole. Close the jump ring. (This is the beginning of the first row.)

2. With an open 20-gauge ³⁄₁₆" jump ring, come up from the back of the bracelet through the third hole and go down through the fourth hole. Close the jump ring.

3. Continue adding 20-gauge ³⁄₁₆" jump rings to complete the first row of the bracelet.

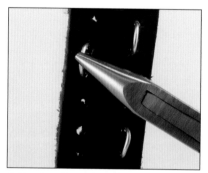 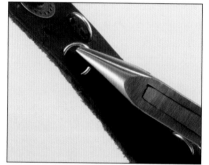

4. On the other side of the bracelet, begin the second row: Skip the first hole and with an open 20-gauge ³⁄₁₆" jump ring come up through the second hole and go down through the third hole. Close the jump ring. This staggers the placement of the jump rings between rows one and two.

5. Continue adding 20-gauge ³⁄₁₆" jump rings to complete the second row of the bracelet. The last hole will not have a jump ring through it.

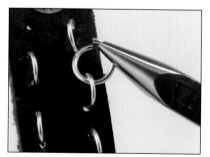 

6. With an open 18-gauge ¹⁵⁄₆₄" jump ring, scoop up the second 20-gauge ³⁄₁₆" jump ring in row one, add three closed 20-gauge ³⁄₃₂" jump rings, and scoop up the first 20-gauge ³⁄₁₆" jump ring in row one. Close the jump ring. Try to keep the three jump rings that you added together along the inside center of the leather blank. If they migrate, don't worry. You can adjust them.

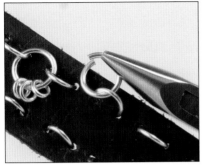

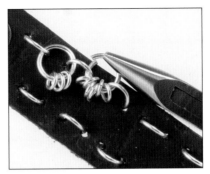

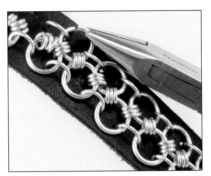

8. Repeat step 7 until the row is completed. When you get to the last jump ring, only add three closed jump rings.

7. With an open 18-gauge ¹⁵⁄₆₄" jump ring, scoop up the third 20-gauge ³⁄₁₆" jump ring in row one, add six closed 20-gauge ³⁄₃₂" jump rings, and scoop up the second 20-gauge ³⁄₁₆" jump ring in row one. Close the jump ring. Be sure that the six jump rings that you added are all together along the center of the leather blank.

9. With an open 18-gauge ¹⁵⁄₆₄" jump ring, and working from the second row of the bracelet, scoop up the first 20-gauge ³⁄₁₆" jump ring, three 20-gauge ³⁄₃₂" jump rings added in step 6, three of the six jump rings added in step 7, and the second 20-gauge ³⁄₁₆" in the row. Close the jump ring.

10. Repeat step 9 to complete the row.

┌─────────────────────────────────────
ANOTHER IDEA

Substitute half-moon rondelle crystals for the 20-gauge ³⁄₃₂" jump rings. The half-moon rondelle crystals add extra bling to an already fabulous bracelet.

PROJECT 11
Club 55 Bracelet

Finished length: 7¾" with extender

WHAT YOU'LL NEED

- **120** 18-gauge ⁷⁄₃₂" jump rings, silver-plated
- **10** 18-gauge ⁹⁄₆₄" jump rings, silver-plated, used for clasp attachment and adjustable clasp point
- lobster claw clasp
- beading awl

This weave uses the concept of *through the eye*. When two jump rings cross over each other it forms what is known as an *eye*. In chain mail theory, the main difference between the European and Persian weave families is the concept of Through the Eye (TE) and Around the Eye (AE) connections. European weaves almost exclusively use TE connections, whereas Persian weaves use both.

● Preparation: Close 33 18-gauge ⁷⁄₃₂" jump rings and Open the remaining. Open all of the 18-gauge ⁹⁄₆₄" jump rings. For illustration, I'm using larger jump rings in different colors for steps 1–12 so you can better see the path and placement of the jump rings.

1. With an open 18-gauge ⁷⁄₃₂" jump ring, scoop up a paperclip and three closed 18-gauge ⁷⁄₃₂" jump rings.

2. Double the jump ring added in step 1.

3. Lay your work down and position it so the three closed jump rings added in step 1 (purple) overlap the two jump rings added in steps 1 and 2 (orange); this creates the eye. Use an awl to define the path.

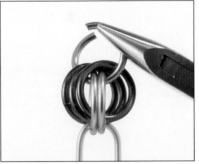

4. With an open 18-gauge ⁷⁄₃₂" jump ring (pink), go through the eye. Close the jump ring.

5. Repeat step 4 twice for a total of three jump rings through the eye (pink).

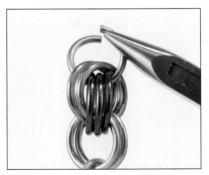

6. With an open 18-gauge ⁷⁄₃₂" jump ring (turquoise), go through the eye created between the three jump rings added in step 1 (purple) and the three jump rings added in steps 4 and 5 (pink). Close the jump ring.

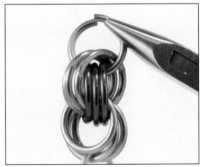

7. Double the jump ring added in step 6.

8. With an open 18-gauge ⁷⁄₃₂" jump ring (orange), scoop up the two jump rings added in steps 6 and 7 (turquoise).

9. Add three closed 18-gauge ⁷⁄₃₂" jump rings (purple). Close the jump ring (orange).

10. Double the jump ring added in steps 8 and 9 (orange).

11. With an open 18-gauge ⁷⁄₃₂" jump ring (pink), go through the eye of the two jump rings added in steps 8 and 10 and the three closed 18-gauge ⁷⁄₃₂" jump rings added in step 9 (purple). Close the jump ring.

12. Triple the jump ring added in step 11 (pink).

13. Repeat steps 6–12 nine times.

14. Repeat steps 6 and 7.

15. With an open 18-gauge ⁹⁄₆₄" jump ring, scoop up the two 18-gauge ⁷⁄₃₂" jump rings added in step 14 and add the lobster claw clasp.

16. Make a chain using the remaining 18-gauge ⁹⁄₆₄" jump rings. I added a five-ring Möbius to the end of my chain. You could also add a charm or just leave it with one jump ring.

17. Remove the paper clip and, with an open 18-gauge ⁹⁄₆₄" jump ring, attach the chain to the bracelet. Close the jump ring.

PROJECT 12
Expandable European 4-in-1 Bracelet

These bracelets are so much fun! Make them in multitudes of colors, and vary the widths. Both the anodized aluminum jump rings and the rubber rings come in a variety of beautiful shades. The best part: There is no need for a clasp!

Finished length: 8"

WHAT YOU'LL NEED

- **51** 15mm rubber rings
- **34** 16-gauge ⅜" anodized aluminum jump rings, turquoise

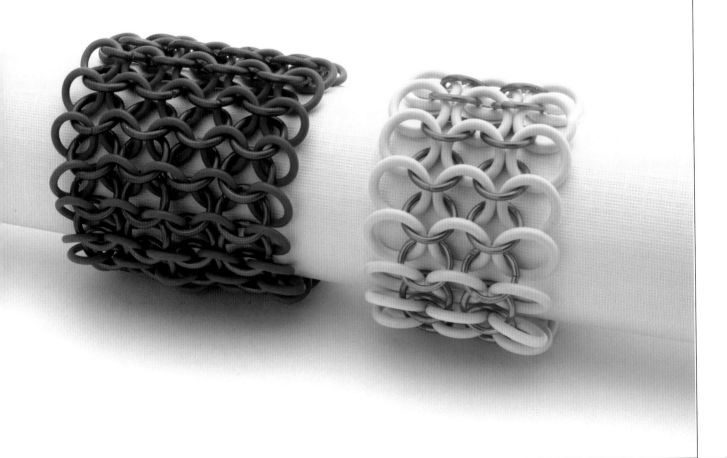

● Preparation: Open all of the turquoise anodized aluminum jump rings. For additional instructions on the European 4-in-1 weave, see Chain Mail Weaves (p. 18).

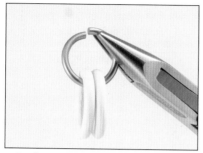

1. With an open turquoise jump ring, scoop up two white rubber rings. Close the turquoise jump ring.

2. With an open turquoise jump ring, scoop up the two white rubber jump rings added in step 1 (scoop up the white rubber rings as you would the two closed jump rings in the original European 4-in-1 weave).

3. Before closing the turquoise jump ring, add two white rubber jump rings. Close the turquoise jump ring.

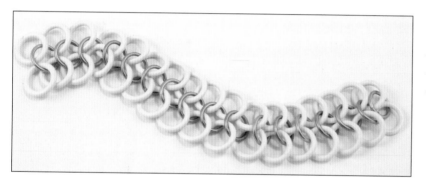

4. Repeat steps 2 and 3 15 more times. Check the fit to be sure the bracelet will fit over the widest part of your hand. Continue the weave, if necessary.

5. This weave is called the 4-in-1 because every turquoise jump ring goes through four white rubber rings. To join the two ends of the weave together to create a circle, you'll join the turquoise jump ring from step 1 (currently passing through two white rubber rings) to the white rings at the other end of the bracelet.

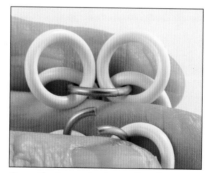

Open the turquoise jump ring from step 1 and scoop up the two end white rubber rings. To make it easier, hold the turquoise jump ring from step 1 between your thumb and second finger, bring the last two white rubber rings around, and hold them between your second and index fingers.

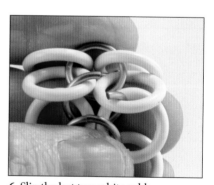

6. Slip the last two white rubber rings onto the open turquoise jump ring as shown.

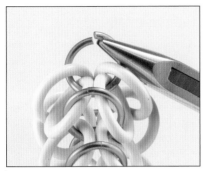

7. Close the turquoise jump ring.

8. To add a second row of turquoise jump rings and an additional single row of white rubber rings: With an open turquoise jump ring, scoop up any two white rubber rings from the right side of the weave.

9. Before closing the turquoise jump ring, add two white rubber rings. Close the turquoise jump ring.

10. Arrange the white rubber jump rings so that they match the pattern of the rest of the bracelet.

11. With an open turquoise jump ring, scoop up the outside white rubber ring, the inside white rubber ring, and the white rubber ring immediately above the white rubber ring.

12. Before closing the turquoise jump ring, add one white rubber ring. Close the turquoise jump ring.

13. Repeat steps 11 and 12 for the length of the bracelet.

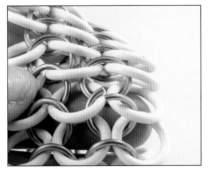

14. With the last turquoise jump ring, scoop up: the white rubber jump ring added in the last step, the white rubber jump ring right next to it, the white rubber jump ring above it, and the first white rubber ring added in this column. Close the turquoise jump ring.

ANOTHER IDEA

Try combining large jump rings with small rubber rings —or small jump rings with large rubber rings—for an interesting look.

PROJECT13
Crystal Washer Bracelet

Finished length: 7¼"

WHAT YOU'LL NEED

- **19** round washers #8
- **42** 18-gauge ¹¹⁄₆₄" jump rings, black
- **19** 3mm crystals, erinite
- Wildfire beading thread, black
- **2** crimp beads, hematite
- lobster and tag clasp, hematite

I found these fabulous washers in our garage. One side of the washer has smooth rounded edges, and the other side has square edges. For this project, I used the smooth rounded edges as the top of my bracelet—but feel free to use either side or mix and match sides for an industrial look.

● **Preparation: Open all of the jump rings.**

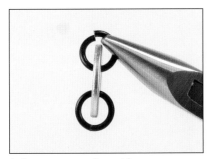

1. Scoop up a washer with an open jump ring. Close the jump ring. Double the jump ring.

2. With an open jump ring, scoop up the clasp and the two jump rings added in step 1. Close the jump ring.

3. With an open jump ring, scoop up the washer from step 1 and a new washer. Close the jump ring. Make sure the new washer lies behind the washer from step 1.

4. Double the jump ring.

5. With an open jump ring, scoop up the washer from step 3 and a new washer. Close the jump ring. Double the jump ring. Make sure the new washer lies on the top of the washer from step 3.

6. Continue adding jump rings and washers, making sure to stagger the placement of the washers.

7. With an open jump ring, scoop up the last two jump rings added and the second half of the clasp. Close the jump ring.

8. String a crimp bead on the beading thread and wrap the working end of the thread around the single jump ring that holds the clasp.

9. With your pliers, flatten the crimp. Trim the tail.

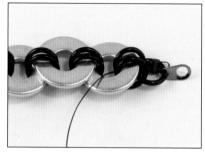

10. Pass the thread between the two jump rings under the washer and out through the center of the washer.

11. String a crystal.

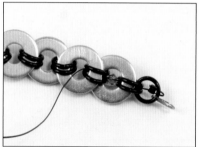

12. Pass the thread over the first washer and under the second washer, always placing it between the two black jump rings. Exit through the center of the second washer.

13. String a crystal.

ANOTHER IDEA

This version of silver-on-silver omits the crystals. To make matching earrings, make a chain using six washers. Join the sixth washer to the first washer, and connect to an earring wire using one 18-gauge ⅛" jump ring.

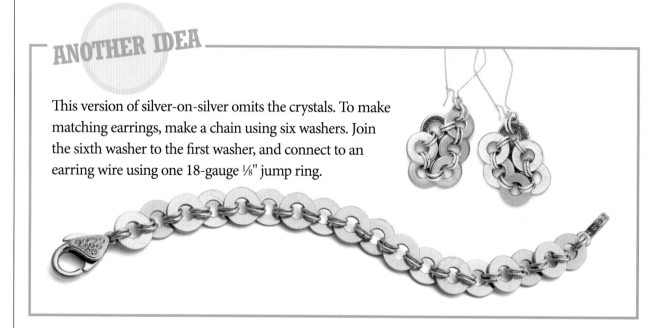

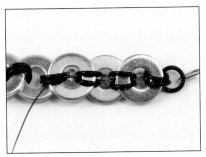

14. Pass the thread under the second washer and over the third washer, always placing it between the two black jump rings. Exit through the center of the third washer.

15. String a crystal.

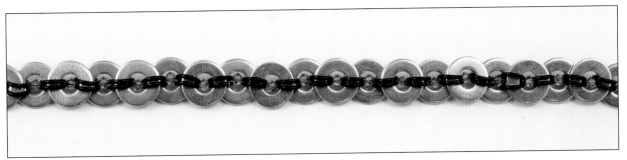

16. Repeat steps 12 and 13 to the end of the bracelet.

17. String a crimp bead. Wrap the thread around the single jump ring that holds the clasp. Crimp the crimp bead and trim the excess thread.

TIP Open your jump rings a bit larger than you normally would. This will make it easier to go around both of the washers.

PROJECT14
Crystal Cross Bracelet

I really enjoy making bracelets and necklaces using the Byzantine weave. However, I also love bling and this Byzantine bracelet combines both!

Finished length: 6¾"

WHAT YOU'LL NEED

- **257** 20-gauge ⁹⁄₆₄" jump rings, silver plated
- **28** 4mm crystals, Swarovski Crystal AB
- **28** ball-tipped headpins, silver plated
- clasp

Wrapped Loop Components
- chainnose pliers
- roundnose pliers
- wire cutters

1. With an open jump ring, scoop up three closed jump rings and the clasp. Close the jump ring.

2. With an open jump ring, scoop up the three closed jump rings from step 1. Close the jump ring.

3. Double the jump ring.

4. With an open jump ring, scoop up the two jump rings added in steps 2 and 3. Close the jump ring.

5. Double the jump ring.

6. Fold down the two jump rings added in steps 4 and 5. See Chain Mail Weaves (p. 20) for complete Byzantine instructions.

7. With an open jump ring, scoop up the inside of the two jump rings folded down in step 6. Close the jump ring.

8. Triple the jump ring.

9. With an open jump ring, scoop up the three jump rings added in steps 7 and 8.

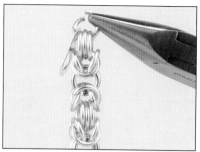

10. Add two closed jump rings. Close the jump ring. Double the jump ring.

11. Repeat steps 6–10 26 more times.

12. Repeat steps 6–8 one time.

13. With an open jump ring, scoop up the three jump rings added in step 12 and the remaining clasp half. Close the jump ring.

ANOTHER IDEA

Make a simple pair of earrings with color! Use an earring wire instead of the clasp in step 1. Make two units of the Byzantine and then add the Möbius to the end of the second Byzantine unit.

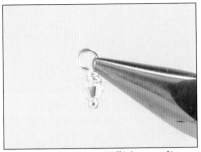

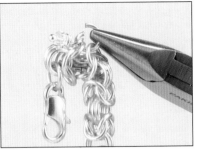

Adding wings or Möbius units

14. Using headpins and crystals, make 28 wrapped-loop components (see Techniques, p. 15, for instructions).

15. Place the bracelet flat on the workspace and notice the position of the Byzantine segments. Where the Byzantine segment was folded over, two jump rings almost touch. Choose two opposite sides of the chain to work on; these will be the jump rings used for attaching the Möbius units.

16. With an open jump ring, scoop up a wrapped-loop component and the two jump rings identified in step 15 on the bracelet. Close the jump ring.

17. With an open jump ring, make a Möbius unit using the same jump rings added in step 16. Be sure to scoop up the wrapped-loop component. Close the jump ring.

18. Repeat steps 16 and 17 for the length of the bracelet (14 additional times).

19. Flip the bracelet over and repeat steps 15–17 on the opposite side of the chain.

TIP When you fold down the two jump rings in step 6, place your thumb and index finger onto the bottom of the jump rings and gently press up. This will make the space to add the next three jump rings easier to see.

PROJECT15
Caterpillar Bracelet

This bracelet combines Parallel, Byzantine, and the Möbius weaves to create a whole new look and dimension. Combining weaves allows you to express your creativity and bring a unique presentation to classic weaves.

Finished length: 8"

WHAT YOU'LL NEED

- **264** 18-gauge $^{15}/_{64}$" jump rings, hematite
- **244** 19-gauge $^{9}/_{64}$" jump rings, pink
- lobster claw clasp with tab, hematite

● Preparation: Open all of the hematite jump rings. Close 104 pink jump rings. Open 140 pink jump rings.

1. With an open hematite jump ring, scoop up two closed pink jump rings and a clasp half. Close the jump ring.

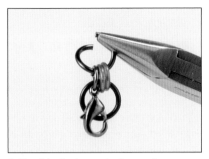

2. Double the hematite jump ring.

3. Continue making a Parallel weave. See Chain Mail Weaves (p. 28) for instructions. Make the Parallel weave 17 double pink jump rings long. End with two hematite jump rings.

4. Scoop up the last two pink jump rings with a hematite jump ring, and add the remaining tab. Close the jump ring.

5. Beginning at the end of the bracelet that has two hematite jump rings, add two pink jump rings. Double the pink jump ring.

6. With an open pink jump ring, scoop up the two pink jump rings added in step 5, and add two closed pink jump rings. Close the pink jump ring.

7. Just like in the instructions for the Byzantine weave (p. 20), fold down the two closed pink jump rings added in step 6.

8. With an open hematite jump ring, scoop up (from the inside) the two closed jump rings from step 6. Close the hematite jump ring.

ANOTHER IDEA

Omit the Parallel portion of the weave and join the Byzantine segments with a three-ring Möbius to create a totally new style of bracelet.

9. With an open hematite jump ring, scoop up the same two pink jump rings you picked up in step 8, and scoop up through the hematite jump ring added in step 8, forming a Möbius by passing the added ring through the center of the first hematite jump ring. Close the hematite jump ring.

10. Add a Byzantine Möbius unit to every double set of hematite jump rings in the Parallel weave.

11. On the other side of the bracelet, add a Byzantine Möbius unit to all of the single hematite jump rings in the Parallel weave.

PROJECT16
Ladder Bracelet

Finished length: 6¾"

WHAT YOU'LL NEED

- **300** 19-gauge ⁵⁄₃₂" enamel coated copper jump rings, lime
- **15** clear eyeglass holders, silver-plated (Beadalon.com)

This bracelet does not require a clasp! You will be creating one unit of Byzantine weave between each circle in the eyeglass holder. Bet you never thought that you would be using eyeglass holders to make bracelets! (For Byzantine Weave instructions, see page 20.)

● **Preparation: Close 120 lime jump rings. Open 180 lime jump rings.**

1. With an open lime jump ring, scoop up two closed lime jump rings and one end of an eyeglass holder. Close the lime jump ring.

2. Double the lime jump ring.

3. Repeat steps 1 and 2 with the same end of the eyeglass holder.

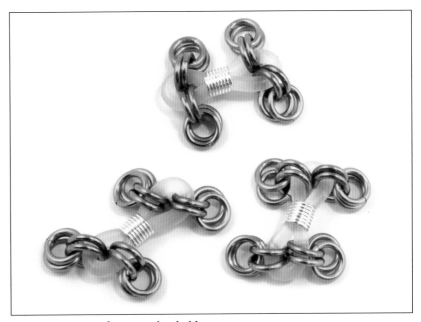

4. Repeat steps 1–3 on the other end of the eyeglass holder.

5. Repeat steps 1–4 for 15 eyeglass holders.

TIP Move the center coil either way to create additional room to add the jump rings. Don't slide the coil all the way off of the rubber ring or it will be very hard to reattach!

6. Fold down the two lime jump rings added in step 1 of one of the set of four lime jump rings on one side of an eyeglass holder.

7. Repeat step 6 with a second eyeglass holder.

8. With an open lime jump ring, scoop up the two closed lime jump rings from step 6 and the two closed lime jump rings from step 7. Close the jump ring.

9. Double the jump ring.

10. Repeat steps 6–9 with all remaining sets of four jump rings. Before linking the final sets, check the fit. Add or remove a component if necessary.

PROJECT 17

Connected Byzantine and Crystal Bracelet

With a little determination and by turning the Byzantine weave on its side, I was finally able to add crystals to a Byzantine bracelet! By now you should realize that I love the bling!

Finished length: 7"

WHAT YOU'LL NEED

- **182** 18-gauge ⁹⁄₆₄" jump rings, peacock blue
- **15** 18-gauge ¼" jump rings, peacock blue
- **58** 11º Japanese seed beads, color to match jump rings
- **13** 4mm bicone crystals, Preciosa 2XAB amethyst
- toggle clasp
- **2** crimp beads
- flexible beading wire, black

● Preparation: Close four 18-gauge %₄" jump rings. Open all remaining 18-gauge %₄" jump rings and all of the 18-gauge ¼" jump rings.

2. Fold back the first two jump rings in the chain.

1. Link 18-gauge %₄" jump rings in a 2-2-2-2-2 chain. Make 15 sets. These will become the Byzantine units you will connect with the 18-gauge ¼" jump rings.

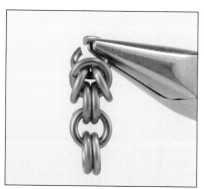

3. With an open 18-gauge %₄" jump ring, scoop up the first two jump rings folded back in step 2.

4. Fold back the last two jump rings in the chain.

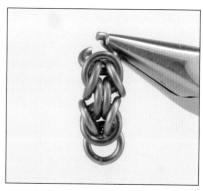

5. With an open 18-gauge %₄" jump ring, scoop up the two folded back jump rings from step 4.

6. Make Byzantine units out of the remaining 15 chains.

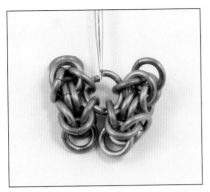

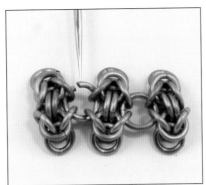

7. With an 18-gauge ¼" jump ring, join two of the Byzantine units by weaving a jump ring through the centermost rings folded over.

8. With an 18-gauge ¼" jump ring, join the two units of Byzantine to a third unit.

9. Continue to connect the Byzantine units until all 15 units are connected. Each end of the bracelet will have an 18-gauge ¼" jump ring only attached to one Byzantine unit.

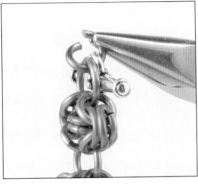

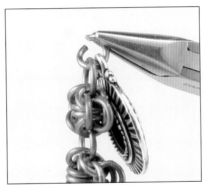

10. Open an 18-gauge %4" jump ring, and scoop up one half of the clasp and the end link of the bracelet.

11. Open an 18-gauge %4" jump ring, and scoop up the remaining clasp half and the remaining end link of the bracelet.

ANOTHER IDEA

Try using larger jump rings to join the Byzantine units for even more sparkle.

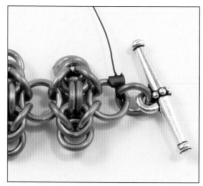  

12. On the beading wire, string a crimp bead and the 18-gauge ⁹⁄₆₄" jump ring added in step 10. Go around the jump ring and back through the crimp bead. Crimp the crimp bead.

13. String five 11° seed beads onto the beading wire and string the beading wire under the two vertical 18-gauge ⁹⁄₆₄" jump rings.

14. String a crystal onto the beading wire.

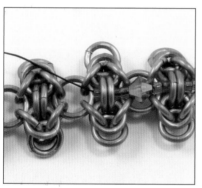  

15. String four 11°s onto the beading wire and string the beading wire under the next two vertical 18-gauge ⁹⁄₆₄" jump rings.

16. Repeat steps 14–15 stopping at step 14 at the last two vertical 18-gauge ⁹⁄₆₄" jump rings.

17. String five 11°s onto the beading wire and then string the beading wire under the last two vertical 18-gauge ⁹⁄₆₄" jump rings. Crimp the end of the beading wire around the 18-gauge ⁹⁄₆₄" jump ring added in step 11 as you did in step 12.

PROJECT18
European 6-in-1 Bracelet

Finished length: 8" with extender

WHAT YOU'LL NEED

- **135** 16-gauge ¼" jump rings, brass
- **94** 16-gauge ¼" jump rings, black
- swivel lobster claw clasp, brass plated

This weave is similar to the European 4-in-1, with one exception—each jump ring goes through six other jump rings instead of only four. (See Chain Mail Weaves for more information about the European 4-in-1, p. 18).

● Preparation: Close 88 black jump rings. Open all of the brass jump rings and six black jump rings.

1. With an open brass jump ring, scoop up the clasp and two closed black jump rings. Close the brass jump ring.

2. Make sure you have mouse ears and a forehead. With an open brass jump ring, scoop up two closed black jump rings added in step 1. Go down through the mouse's right ear, around the back of his forehead, and back up through his left ear. Close the brass jump ring.

3. From now on, instead of picking up one set of the mouse's ears, you will be picking up two. With an open brass jump ring, scoop up two closed black jump rings. Go down through two of the mouse's right ears around the back of his forehead and back up through his two left ears. Close the brass jump ring.

4. Repeat step 3 for the length of the bracelet.

ANOTHER IDEA

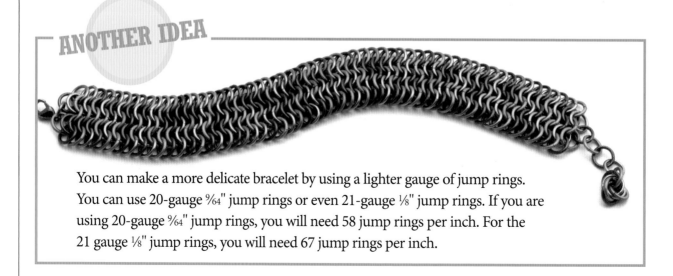

You can make a more delicate bracelet by using a lighter gauge of jump rings. You can use 20-gauge ⁹⁄₆₄" jump rings or even 21-gauge ¹⁄₈" jump rings. If you are using 20-gauge ⁹⁄₆₄" jump rings, you will need 58 jump rings per inch. For the 21 gauge ¹⁄₈" jump rings, you will need 67 jump rings per inch.

Finishing the other end of the bracelet

5. With an open brass jump ring, add a closed black jump ring and scoop up the last two black jump rings added in step 4. Close the brass jump ring.

6. With an open brass jump ring, add a closed black jump ring and attach it to the closed black jump ring from step 5. Close the brass jump ring.

7. Repeat step 6. I added a Möbius to the end of my bracelet. You can choose to add a Möbius or a charm, or leave the chain plain.

Making the bracelet wider

8. Beginning on the right side of the bracelet (or the mouse's right ears) with an open brass jump ring, scoop up the first three right ears. Close the brass jump ring.

9. With an open brass jump ring, scoop up the fourth mouse ear, the third mouse ear, and the second mouse ear. Close the brass jump ring. Each brass jump ring you add will lie behind the previous brass jump ring.

10. Repeat step 9 all the way down the right side of the bracelet.

11. Flip the bracelet over. With an open brass jump ring, scoop up the mouse's first three ears. Close the brass jump ring.

12. With an open brass jump ring, scoop up the fourth mouse ear, the third mouse ear, and the second mouse ear. Close the brass jump ring. Each brass jump ring you add will lie in front of the previous brass jump ring.

13. Repeat step 12 all the way down the right side of the bracelet.

Glossary

Alloy: A combination of elements: A metal alloy combines a metal with one or more other metals or non-metals to enhance its properties.

Aluminum: A chemical element and the third most common element on the planet, aluminum is soft, durable, and lightweight. Aluminum jump rings are available in a wide range of colors and sizes.

American Wire Gauge: Also known as Brown & Sharpe, American Wire Gauge is used to determine the wire diameter of precious metals.

Argentium sterling silver: Argentium is 92.5% silver and the other 7.5% is copper and metalloid germanium. Germanium is a lustrous, hard, grayish-white metalloid element which decreases oxidizing or tarnishing. Argentium silver is harder than sterling silver.

Aspect ratio: Referred to as AR, it describes the relationship between the wire gauge and the inner diameter of the ring, and determines how airy or tight a weave is. The formula to calculate the aspect ratio is the inner diameter of a jump ring divided by the wire diameter. AR is important when changing the scale of a weave.

Base metals: Non-precious metals including aluminum, copper, brass, bronze, and stainless steel.

Bronze: An alloy made from copper and other metals (usually tin). Often yellow in color, it can look like shiny gold.

Brass: An alloy made from copper and zinc.

Copper: An element. Pure copper is soft and malleable, so it is usually combined with other elements to create strength.

Diameter: The length of any straight-line segment that passes through the center of the circle and whose endpoints are on the boundary of the circle. In chain mail, the most common measurement for jump rings is the inside diameter. Inside diameter is important in calculating aspect ratio.

Doubling a jump ring: Adding another jump ring in exactly the same size, next to the original jump ring, and passing through exactly the same rings as the first jump ring.

Enamel-coated wire: Copper or aluminum wire coated with a very thin layer of colored enamel.

Fine silver: 99.9% silver; very soft and malleable and not recommended for use in making chain mail jump rings.

German silver: Also known as nickel silver, it is typically made up 60% copper, 20% nickel, and 20% zinc. Knowing the content is important when considering nickel allergies. German silver contains no elemental silver unless plated.

Kerf: The cut in the jump ring where the saw blade sliced through the metal.

Mandrel: A cylindrical form (usually steel). Wind wire on a mandrel to create a coil used to make jump rings. Determines the inside diameter of the jump ring.

Niobium: A hypoallergenic wire which is electrically heated and anodized resulting in a wide array of colors. Take care when using these jump rings to avoid damage to the color. It is helpful to apply painters tape or a rubberized coating such as Tool Magic to your pliers.

Pinch-out or pinch-cut: Jump rings that are cut using wire cutters or flush cutters are often referred to as "pinch-out" or "pinch-cut" jump rings. Because of the way that wire cutters are made, one side of the jaws is usually flat or "flush" and the other side has an angle that looks similar to this: <. The resulting jump ring cut is flat on one side and pinched on the other. You can never completely close the jump ring.

Precious metal: A rare, naturally occurring metallic chemical element such as silver, gold, or platinum.

Saw cut: A cut in the jump ring that results in both edges of the jump ring being flush or flat. This enables perfect closure on a jump ring. Saw-cut jump rings are the jump rings jewelry makers like to use.

Silver: A precious metal. Common forms of silver are fine silver (99.9% pure), sterling silver (92.5% pure), and Argentium silver (92.5% pure).

Silver filled: This term can be misleading. It means that sterling silver is bonded to or over a core of brass. There are different thicknesses of sterling silver overlay, including $\frac{1}{10}$" and $\frac{1}{20}$". Silver-filled wire is becoming extremely popular due to its inexpensive cost.

Silver plated: Usually has a copper core surrounded by a very thin (thinner than silver filled) layer of silver.

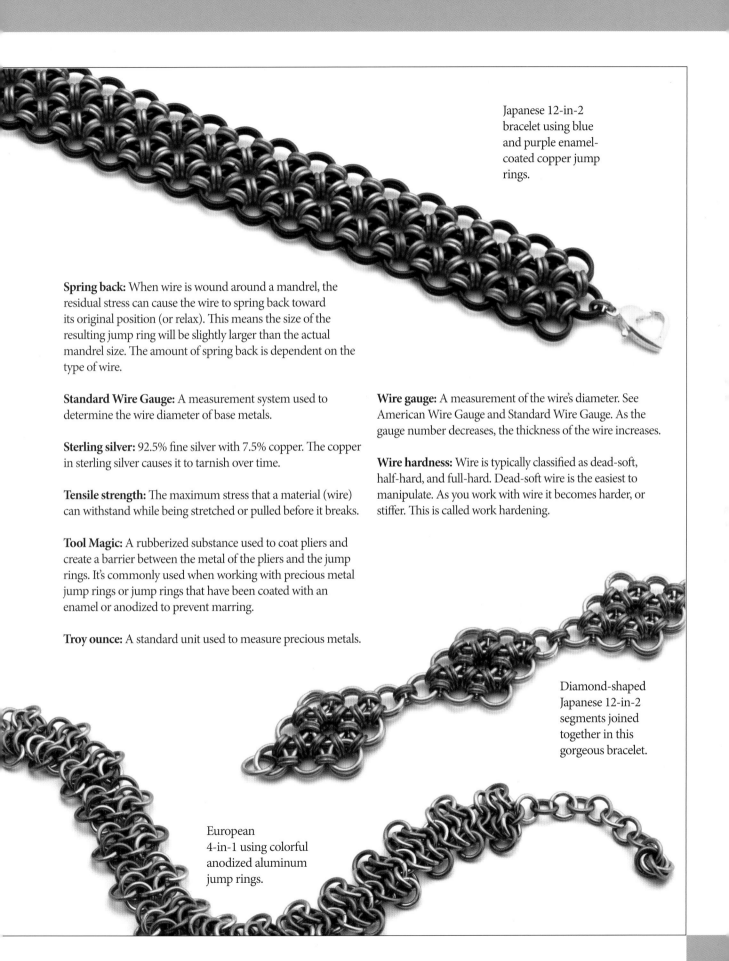

Japanese 12-in-2 bracelet using blue and purple enamel-coated copper jump rings.

Spring back: When wire is wound around a mandrel, the residual stress can cause the wire to spring back toward its original position (or relax). This means the size of the resulting jump ring will be slightly larger than the actual mandrel size. The amount of spring back is dependent on the type of wire.

Standard Wire Gauge: A measurement system used to determine the wire diameter of base metals.

Sterling silver: 92.5% fine silver with 7.5% copper. The copper in sterling silver causes it to tarnish over time.

Tensile strength: The maximum stress that a material (wire) can withstand while being stretched or pulled before it breaks.

Tool Magic: A rubberized substance used to coat pliers and create a barrier between the metal of the pliers and the jump rings. It's commonly used when working with precious metal jump rings or jump rings that have been coated with an enamel or anodized to prevent marring.

Troy ounce: A standard unit used to measure precious metals.

Wire gauge: A measurement of the wire's diameter. See American Wire Gauge and Standard Wire Gauge. As the gauge number decreases, the thickness of the wire increases.

Wire hardness: Wire is typically classified as dead-soft, half-hard, and full-hard. Dead-soft wire is the easiest to manipulate. As you work with wire it becomes harder, or stiffer. This is called work hardening.

Diamond-shaped Japanese 12-in-2 segments joined together in this gorgeous bracelet.

European 4-in-1 using colorful anodized aluminum jump rings.

Hints

■ When working with plated or enamel-coated jump rings, you can see where the jump ring is joined because of the copper core.

■ The larger the wire gauge, the thinner the wire.

■ Keep your clasps closed until you have attached both ends of the bracelet or necklace. This will ensure that the clasp is attached correctly.

■ The triangular scoop is great for scooping up the jump rings and returning them to their compartments.

■ The triangular scoop is great for counting jump rings. Place your jump rings on the beading mat and use the tip of the tray to count and separate rings from a pile.

■ Copy and laminate the two charts (p. 12), and carry them with you when you shop for chain mail jump rings.

■ When attaching clasps and weaves to earring wires, I use the smallest jump ring that I can. I find that this helps to "show off" your design. Larger jump rings tend to be distracting.

■ When determining the size to make a bracelet, always include the size of the clasp in your measurement. I usually allow ½" for the clasp. Example: when making a 7" bracelet, the weave portion will be 6½" and the clasp will be ½".

■ When making a wrapped loop, take care in wrapping the wire around the stem; over wrapping may result in damage to the bead or crystal.

■ When you get a new pair of pliers, take time to sand the edges of the jaws with a fine piece of sanding paper or emery tool. You don't need a lot of sanding—just enough to "soften" the edge.

■ After peeling Tool Magic from your pliers, hit the jaws with a bit of sanding. The jaws tend to be a bit slippery after an application of Tool Magic.

■ Removing tape from the jaws of your pliers will leave them sticky. Remove this stickiness with peanut butter or Goo Gone.

■ Make sure that the pliers you use have tension springs or return springs. Some pliers come with adjustable tension springs.

■ I always recommend that beginners purchase pre-made jump rings.

■ Buy inexpensive jump rings, such as copper or aluminum, for practicing. When you are confident with your abilities, move on to using precious metal jump rings.

■ Always open your jump rings by *twisting* the ends apart. Never open a jump ring by *pulling* the ends apart.

■ Opening and closing a jump ring too many times will cause the jump ring to become brittle and eventually break.

Acknowledgments

I would like to thank my wonderful, loving, and supportive husband, Shan. If not for his encouragement and brute strength I would not be where I am today. He supported my work from the very beginning. Every Friday night, he unpacked our SUV, put up the tent, and sat with me for hours selling my jewelry at our local farmers market. We did this for over a year before we ventured indoors to major bead shows. Thank you, honey, for allowing me to have a whole room in the house for my chain mail obsession and putting up with jump rings all over the house. (You would be surprised where we find those pesky jump rings!)

I wish to thank my fabulous editor, Karin Van Voorhees, for all of her hard work, patience, and wonderful editing skills. Thank you also to Kalmbach Books for believing me and giving me this chance to share my passion with others.

Thank you Miss Gizmo, our adorable little Chihuahua, for lying in my lap and keeping me company during the writing of this book and allowing me to lay my chain mail tray on you while you slept.

And finally I would like to thank all of my wonderful students who have taught me so much over the last few years. I love it when I'm teaching and suddenly the light bulb goes on and my students "get it"!

About the Author

Lauren was born and raised in beautiful southern California. She was blessed with having an extremely talented and crafty mother. Her father was an equally talented civil engineer. Lauren holds degrees in accounting, paralegal studies, and pharmacy technician. (She couldn't decide what she wanted to be when she grew up!) Most of her career was spent being "serious." Now is the fun part of her life! She loves taking a raw material, like wire, and turning it into a gorgeous new creation. She also loves to bead, macramé, and do various forms of needlepoint.

Lauren has been weaving tiny jump rings for over seven years now. She teaches classes in chain mail at her local bead shops and also at various craft shows. She loves teaching and sharing her passion with others. Lauren is honored to be a member of the Beadalon Design Team. In addition to supporting her designing habit, Beadalon has been instrumental in Lauren's frequent guest appearances on the popular television series *Beads, Baubles, and Jewels* and Jewelry Television's *Jewel School.*

Visit Lauren's website to find chain mail jump rings, tools, books, finished chain mail jewelry, and more: TheChainMailleLady.com.

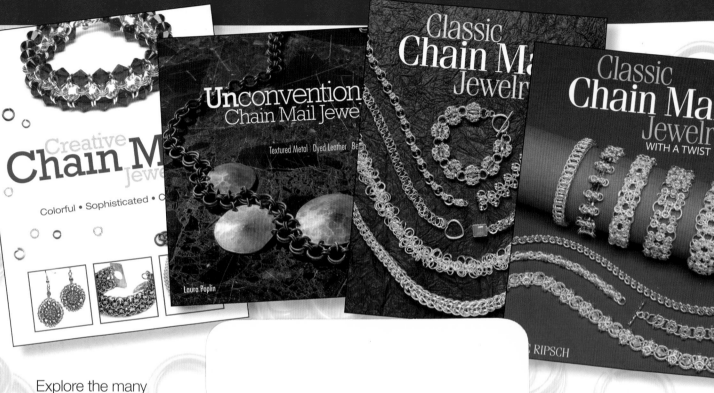

745.5942 ANDERSEN

Discard

Andersen, Lauren.
Making chain mail jewelry

NWEST

R4000382151

NORTHWEST
Atlanta-Fulton Public Library

–533-6644

8776, ext. 661.